WHAT AMERICA LOST:
DECADES THAT MADE A
DIFFERENCE

Tracking Attitude Changes Through Handwriting

Sallie Ferrell Bolich

authorHOUSE®

AuthorHouse™
1663 Liberty Drive
Bloomington, IN 47403
www.authorhouse.com
Phone: 1-800-839-8640

First published by AuthorHouse 10/19/2009

ISBN: 978-1-4389-7500-9 (sc)

Library of Congress Control Number: 2009903843

Printed in the United States of America
Bloomington, Indiana

This book is printed on acid-free paper.

ACKNOWLEDGEMENTS

Thank you to everyone who so willingly took time to copy pages of yearbook messages, discuss and make them available to me. Without your efforts this study would not have been possible.

Thank you to Larry Vorwerck, for all of his computer expertise and hours of work.

Thank you to my husband, Don, for his continued support and assistance with day to day living.

This book is dedicated to the memory of our son, Steve, who shared my belief in handwriting analysis. While studying for his MBA, Steve presented a paper, "Graphoanalysis and Personnel Selection."

CONTENTS

INTRODUCTION   xi

CHAPTER I

History Of Handwriting Analysis   1

CHAPTER II

A New Slant On Life   5
  Measuring Slant in Handwriting   5

    •   Simplified Slant Measuring Gauge   6
  Understanding the Variances of Slant   6
  Nature vs. Nurture   8
  The Big Emotional Shift   8

    •   Transition of Handwriting Slant   9
  The Fifties Decade   10
  The Sixties Decade   12
  The Seventies Decade   15
  The Eighties Decade   17
  The Nineties Decade   18

    •   Handwriting Slant Shift 1959 vs 1990   21

CHAPTER III

What Handwriting Size Reveals   25
    •   Transition of Handwriting Size   28
    •   Handwriting Size Shift   33

CHAPTER IV

Do We Have A Mundane Reality?   37
  The Written Script—Expression of Self   38

    •   Transition from Abstract to Mundane   40
  The Fifties Decade   41
  The Sixties Decade   44

The Seventies Decade   46
The Eighties Decade   47
The Nineties Decade   48

   • Decline of Abstract Thinking   51

CHAPTER V

Are You Raising The Bar?   55

   • Transition of Goal Setting   58

   • Shift in Goal setting   61

CHAPTER VI

Pride Taketh A Fall   65
Independent Thinking   66

   • Transition of Personal Pride Letter d   68

   • Transition of Pride in Performance Letter t   69
The Fifties Decade   70
The Sixties Decade   72
The Seventies Decade   73
The Eighties Decade   75
The Nineties Decade   76

   • Increase in Independent Thinking Letter d   80

   • Increase in Independent Thinking Letter t   81

CHAPTER VII

Society's Missing Links   85

   • Decline in Generosity   89

CHAPTER VIII

The Self-Esteem Puzzle   93
    Do Struggles Hinder or Help?   95
    Self-Esteem Cannot be Bought   97
    Can The Newer Approach Succeed?   97

      • Decline in Self Esteem   99

CHAPTER IX

Styles Have Changed!   103
    The Decline of Penmanship   104
    The Importance of Penmanship   105
    What Does Printing Mean to the Handwriting Analyst?   106

      • Changes in Writing Style   108

CHAPTER X

Is The Handwriting On The Wall?   109
    A Glimpse into the Future   110
    Change Continues   111
    A New Outlook Sets Our Course   112
    Assessing Our Course   114

BIBLIOGRAPHY   115

ABOUT THE AUTHOR   119

INTRODUCTION

For centuries, people have been intrigued by handwriting analysis—how it can reveal so much about one's personality. It's a wonderful instrument for better understanding yourself and others you interact with, provided you have a solid, proven system behind you. My background as a Certified Graphoanalyst, a handwriting analyst, has given me the opportunity to share personality insights with many people.

Graphoanalysis is a specific empirically researched system of handwriting analysis developed in America. I received my certification from the International Graphoanalysis Society, (formerly located in Chicago, Illinois) of New Kensington, Pennsylvania. For the past 20 years I have employed my knowledge in my consulting service in Broomfield, Colorado, working with businesses, mental health professionals, and private individuals.

In the spring of 1996, I was invited to speak to several psychology classes at a high school in the Denver suburbs. As part of my talk, handwriting samples were requested from students so that I could tell them something about their potential to achieve their goals. The classes were composed of seniors, who soon would be graduating and entering the world as adults. As I reviewed over 100 samples, I noted that the majority of students were struggling with feelings of self-underestimation (doubting their abilities), and mistrust as they viewed relationships and faced the future.

This was not what I had expected their writing to show. Here was a new generation with the advantage of a superior education. School curricula had been revised to include such studies as success in relationships, developing self-esteem, and conflict resolution. I had thought that these graduates would be better prepared to enter the world than my generation, graduates of the 1950s. Instead, the majority of the writing samples showed that goal setting was not ambitious. Most of the samples showed the goals were immediate, reflecting day-to-day concerns only. Enthusiasm was missing, and their approach to life was more emotionally controlled than I had expected.

These findings were puzzling. After all, isn't graduation the culmination of years of schoolwork—giving young people a chance to finally use their skills and become independent? After high school, a graduate is ready to pursue goals and plan for the future as an adult, right? I had expected to see trait indications showing higher goals and enthusiasm.

But since there was no evidence of this, I thought that perhaps this period, just prior to graduation, could be a very unsettling one for teens. Maybe high school graduation is a time when one doesn't feel confident enough to set high goals. Perhaps graduates are overwhelmed with the choices they face and the decisions to be made. The teenage years can be extremely difficult for many, which may explain why these traits of self-underestimation and mistrust were prevalent in the writings I was studying.

I tried to recall the feelings I had when I was a senior, less than two months from graduation. Did I have these feelings of self-underestimation and caution? How did my classmates view their futures? I remember feeling uncertain, while knowing I could rely on my inner resources and turn to others for help if necessary. I do not remember feeling mistrust or caution as I thought of the future. There were some feelings of anxiety about leaving home and going away to college in another state, but the idea of doing this was also exciting. My classmates and I were anxious to graduate; the world was there for us, as high school graduates, to experience and enjoy.

As a way of confirming my theory, relative to self-underestimation and mistrust, I checked into several 1950s-era senior yearbooks. Handwritten messages would show how seniors of that time viewed the future and their level of trust. The samples from the 1950s proved to be very different from those taken in 1996. These 50s samples showed a more settled approach to life. Why was I seeing profound changes in certain traits revealed in the handwriting? My belief was that they reflect the many changes that took place in our society during this almost 50-year period.

While less time spent on penmanship drills might account for an increase of writing in the printed form and the decline of penmanship, it does not explain the percentage of changes in specific handwriting strokes. These strokes, or indicators within the written letters, reveal vital personality traits to the handwriting analyst. The analyst carefully assesses these traits and weighs them against each other in order to determine the character and personality of the writer.

After comparing handwriting of the 50s with samples from 1996, I decided to begin a study, comparing any changes decade by decade. This study would be limited to high school seniors living in the suburbs. Gathering hundreds of writing samples from senior yearbooks between 1950 and 2000, I compiled my data. I chose to study those traits that would reveal the attitudes of graduates as they prepared to enter this new, independent period in their lives. Would it be possible to correlate handwriting changes with societal changes that would influence the writer's perspective on life? I thought so. Societal attitudes, values taught, standards held, and lifestyles all influence who we are as adults. Handwriting reveals the character, personality and mental attitude of the writer. It is a window on the true inner person, and I thought it would show how societal changes have shaped young people's attitudes.

The identification of seven significant traits found in every handwriting revealed how changes in societal standards and values had influenced behavior; recorded handwriting changes reflected this. The trait indicators in writing showed a decline in pride, long-range planning, self-esteem, goal-setting, and trust in the minds of young people, as well as an increase in self-absorption. This text gives the untrained reader a basic understanding of how handwriting analysis is used to gauge personal development. Attitudes and outlooks result from influence of parents, schools, friends and the culture.

The trend in societal changes began in the late 1950s and continued over the next 50 years. Since then we have seen many changes—in patterns of behavior, of philosophies, and expectations. Societal standards, expectations, and behavioral norms create an environment for our youth, and they become a product of the times in which they live. Regardless of efforts to resist these changes, these influences are felt and have a profound effect on the minds of young people.

As a result of these 50 years of change, the patterns of behavior, philosophies and expectations a high school graduate in the 90's held differed greatly from that of a 50's graduate.

While students in the study are individual personalities and their life experiences differ; there is a common thread that makes them unique to their generation. They become a product of the times.

Knowledge of handwriting analysis gives us an understanding of how societal attitudes, values and lifestyles influence our thinking. Handwriting analysis serves as a window to the inner person.

Chapter I

HISTORY OF HANDWRITING ANALYSIS

Graphology is the term covering the analysis of personality from handwriting. *Webster's Dictionary* calls it a study of handwriting, especially to define character and aptitudes. The on-line *Encyclopedia Britannica* calls it an inference of character from a person's handwriting. The theory underlying graphology is that handwriting is an expression of personality.

The term comes from the Greek words *graphein*, to write and *logos*, the science of. Graphoanalysis is a separate, copyrighted system of graphology, developed in the United States in the early twentieth century by M.N. Bunker.

There are records of written communication dating back 6,000 years. It was accomplished by drawing or carving symbols into stone or clay. In 1000 B.C., the educated few in Japan were studying the formation of the bars in script as a way to judge character. The first known statement regarding a correlation between personality and handwriting occurred when Emperor Nero pointed out a man in court and said, "His writing shows him to be treacherous." The Roman historian Tranquillus noted that the mean spirit of Caesar Augustus could be told from the tightness of his writing.

During the Middle Ages, monks were the only ones who practiced this skill. However, during the Renaissance handwriting interested the intellectuals, bringing more awareness to this study. Shakespeare is supposed to have said, "Give me the handwriting of a woman and I will tell you her character."

Serious study of handwriting analysis actually began in Europe in the 1600s. In 1622, Camillo Baldi, a professor at the University of Bologna, published a book detailing a method of revealing the nature of a person through a study of his handwriting. His publication, entitled *A Treatise on a Method to Recognize the Nature and Quality of a Writer*

From His Letters, attracted the interest of many, especially entertainers. Groups of entertainers then traveled from castle to castle, doing character interpretations for people based on their handwriting. The entertainment became very popular but was limited to a few because most people could not read or write, so it did not gain much recognition.

Early in the 18th century, educated litterateur and critic Baron de Grimm, brought more awareness of handwriting analysis to the educated upper class. At this time, graphology began to earn status as something more than just a parlor game.

Around 1830 Baldi's technique was studied by clergy in the Catholic Church. In France, two priests, Abbe Louis J. H. Flandrin and the Archbishop of Cambri, began a serious study of thousands of handwriting specimens. Their assistant, Abbe Jean-Hippolyte Michon, made the most significant contribution when he attached a definite meaning to each graphic sign. This method was known as "the school of fixed signs." In 1875, Abbe Michon published his work, *Systeme de graphologie*, thus beginning the graphology movement in Europe. By the end of the nineteenth century, an intense study of handwriting analysis had begun. Many French and German scholars began researching this field.

Crepieux-Jamin, a student of Abbe Michon's, convinced psychologist Alfred Binet to use graphology as a technique for personality testing. Binet's experiments resulted in an accuracy rating from 61% to 92%, very high considering the crude methods that were being used.

In Germany, Wilhelm Preyer conducted many university experiments and hypothesized that "all writing is brain writing." A German chemist, Ludwig Klages, became most well known in the field of handwriting analysis as he used his findings to add to the knowledge of his predecessors. His research led him to realize that the stresses, rhythms and experiences that a person deals with on a daily basis have a style consistent with motor behavior and the rhythm of movement. He used the term "expressive movement" in theorizing that in handwriting the movement between these forces comes together. Klages' work was not followed widely; instead it was mainly confined to Germany (the place for science circles at that time), because many scholars questioned the validity of his system.

It wasn't till the early part of the 20th century that Graphology began to gain recognition in the United States. At the University of

Wyoming, psychology professor June Downey realized the value of handwriting analysis in her field. In 1919, she published *Graphology and the Psychology of Handwriting.*

In the meantime, another educator interested in handwriting analysis, M. N. Bunker, was teaching shorthand classes in Springfield, MO. For some time, he had observed that his students kept making deviations from the shorthand strokes he taught; each student formed their own style. While borrowing on the theories of European graphology, he began doing his own research to see what really worked in analyzing writing.

Enlisting the help of students and other interested parties, he accumulated thousands of handwriting samples. He discussed the writing characteristics he found with the writers. Devoting countless hours to research using empirical methods, he made the discovery that it was the "stroke"—the portion of the letter rather than the whole letter—that indicated personality traits. He was urged to make his system available to the public, and he did so beginning in 1929. In Graphoanalysis, the slant, size, and pressure of the writing are considered, along with stroke indications of 125 personality traits.

In addition to stroke indications, Bunker also taught that one had to consider the influence of other traits in the personality that would have an intensifying or reductive effect on the expression of a given trait. For example, a person might have a desire to be talkative—to share her real ideas and feelings—but if other traits made her inhibited, then one could conclude that she might not talk because she was afraid to. This important concept is called *evaluation*, and it is necessary to produce an accurate picture of the personality as it is expressed.

In 1929, Bunker founded the International Graphoanalysis Society (IGAS) which is still in operation today. The study is offered by correspondence and requires testing to receive certification. Certified Graphoanalysts come from all walks of life. They are consulted to help in business, industry, mental health clinics, genealogy (learning what one's ancestors were really like) as well as for personal analysis, to gain insight for self-understanding.

The Society, which has members in every state and abroad, can be reached through its website, *www.igas.com*

Chapter II

A NEW SLANT ON LIFE

It is most important to understand what the **slant** of handwriting means, and how that affects the writer's personality. **Slant** is often the first trait an analyst considers when studying a handwriting sample.

Does the writing slant forward, backward, or is it straight up and down? For complete accuracy, the analyst uses a gauge to determine the degrees of slant in a specimen. To simplify things, we will "eyeball" the slant of our specimens.

The slant of the writing indicates the varying degrees of the writer's emotional responsiveness. How hard do emotions hit us? Are we high-strung, cool-headed, or withdrawn? Strong responsiveness means that our emotions are aroused intensely, and in a wide range of situations. We have many impulses to deal with; they sway our judgment. However, a person with low responsiveness feels little emotional arousal, so one's judgment easily prevails. Emotions are often called the cornerstone of the personality. No matter how one controls the expression of emotions felt, this internal arousal affects all personality traits. Because of this, emotional responsiveness is considered one of the factors which has a profound, personality-wide influence. As an individual encounters more of life's experiences *writing slant can change if the writer tries to control responsiveness, an act of self-protection.*

Measuring Slant in Handwriting

We measure slant by drawing a base line under each letter, and then we draw a line between two points, the first is where the upstroke leaves the base line and the second point is the highest point of that upstroke. A line is then drawn to connect these two points—this line is known as a slant line. **Only upstrokes are measured in determining slant**. To determine the degree of emotional responsiveness these slant lines are measured with a gauge. For simplification, in this study, the handwriting slant has been condensed to four basic categories. The following is an illustration of a simplified gauge used to measure the slant lines drawn. This illustration will aid the untrained eye to see how the slant of handwriting (the direction of writing) varies. This direction, referred to as the slant, affects the writer's deeply felt level of responsiveness as he/she reacts to situations, to other people.

Simplified Slant Measuring Gauge

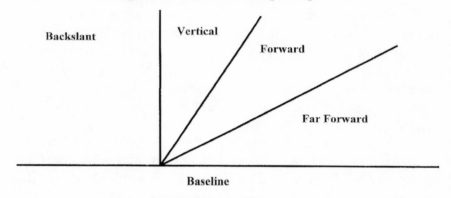

Four Categories of Slant

Understanding the Variances of Slant
BACKSLANT

Forward movement, to the right of the paper, is our natural direction. Backslanted writing moves to the left instead, this is not natural—and it doesn't mean the writers are left-handed. This slant shows that these individuals have been considerably hurt in the past, or greatly imposed upon. Therefore, as soon as something makes them feel insecure, they become cool and distant, put themselves first, and seem unable to express their real feelings at the time.

Even though backslanted writers are often outgoing and friendly, perhaps even be the life of the party, these people are not completely able to trust others however, because of what has happened to them in the past. It is possible for adolescents to show some occasional backslant in their writing, as growing up has its stresses and strains. Backslanted writing indicates a tendency to pull back when feeling insecure. Many years ago, when left-handed children were forced to write with their right hands, a backslant sometimes resulted from this trauma. Caution has replaced spontaneity that comes with a forward leaning slant.

VERTICAL SLANT

thank

This writing category has a mix of very little to a mild slant. The vertical writing means that objectivity rules, even in emergencies, with apparently no emotions present. A mild slant means a mild emotional inclination which is easily overcome as the head rules the heart.

The logic and judgment of the vertical writer will result in a cool, poised response to situations. This logic and judgment can make one seem like Star Trek's "Mister Spock," who frequently used the word "logical"—if it wasn't based on pure logic, it didn't seem right to him. This emotional approach can seem uncaring, even unfriendly.

Writing with a mild slant to the right could be considered a "golden mean" showing a balance of emotion and judgment. There is some outgoing tendency, but because the responses are weaker, they are not hard to control. These writers have developed this control on their responsiveness as a guard against being vulnerable.

Handwriting slant measurements of the fifties showed only **17.9%** of graduates fell into this less responsive, less trusting category, while samples of students in the nineties revealed an astonishing increase, or **72.0%**.

FORWARD SLANT

thank

These writers feel warm, sympathetic responses to situations, though they don't like to feel they are being swept away by emotions. While these writers feel empathic and readily respond, they like to "keep one foot on the base of judgment." They are able to curb their emotions, refrain from reacting intensely while still experiencing involvement with an outward expression of caring.

FAR FORWARD SLANT

thank

The people with a strong forward lean to their writing are high-keyed, feeling many intense emotions in a wide range of situations. They live with impulses, and as a result really need traits that will restrain too-quick expression of their emotions. Their thinking is so strongly influenced by emotion that they must guard against "thinking with their heart and not their head."

Unless they are restrained, they show their feelings readily and are quick to empathize. They can appear warm and friendly, and connect with others quickly. These writers have the potential to lead others with emotional appeals, and they will be on the front line of response when there is a need for help.

Nature vs. Nurture

Today science is learning more and more about genetic and environmental influences on personality. Many years ago, Milton Bunker, the founder of Graphoanalysis, noticed that children seemed to be born with different degrees of responsiveness. Still, we have to consider that the many experiences that occur to one during childhood and even into adult life influence one's responsiveness.

If people's security is threatened in their young years or even later, they can lose their normal degree of responsiveness in favor of gaining control of their feelings. And as we have said, if they have been "burned" in some way they can become ready to emotionally withdraw, shown by the shift to a more vertical or backward slant in their writing.

The Big Emotional Shift

Slant percentages during this fifty-year period show a great change. The fifties samples showed predominately responsive natures, with the far forward category scoring **68.1%.** On the other hand, nineties samples showed only **5.6%.** This represents a **62.5%** decline in responsiveness, reflecting a startling increase in caution as teens reach out to others. It's interesting to note how Generation X and Generation Y view involvement with others; their approach is much more restrained than students of the fifties.

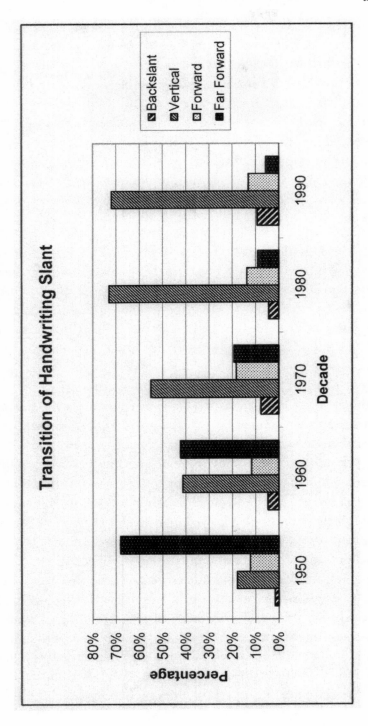

This data can be better understood as we review many sociological events over that fifty-year span, and see how they correlate with changes in handwriting. Society and personal experiences have a great impact on who we become and perceptions we have.

Graduates in the nineties, including the year 2000, spent their childhood in the late seventies, eighties and early nineties. They experienced a very different world than the students who grew up in the late thirties, forties and fifties, graduating during the fifties. Let's take a look at the events of the different decades and define how these events and societal attitudes could have affected security, a willingness to trust.

The Fifties Decade

For those families who joined the popular migration, from the city to a new house in the suburbs, the fifties was a time of opportunity and security. The country was experiencing a growing economic market and an unchallenged belief that our country was a leader in the world. Suburbanites felt united as they worked together to achieve a better life for their families. Strong bonds between people gave a secure atmosphere for the majority of young people.

The growing middle class was able to enjoy these rewards after enduring sacrifices and hard times during World War II. The country was very united, with the goal of building a better life for their children and working together for the greater good. Children were taught to help others and to practice the Golden Rule—"Do unto others as you would have them do unto you." Idealism prevailed as children were raised to believe that if they played by the rules and worked hard, all would turn out well. This guideline was taught in home, at church and school, and it built feelings of trust and connection.

High school or college graduates of the fifties felt more secure and confident than at any other time in our nation's history as they entered the work force. When graduates went to work for a company and decided on a career there, the assumption was that the job would last until retirement. The financial future was secure if employees had a steady work record; the company's pension plan would take care of them in retirement. The financially solvent Social Security system provided benefits. Most corporations were solid, established entities, and future employment was guaranteed. A handshake and a promise was usually all that was necessary to cement many business dealings. The popular belief was that "a man's word is his honor." This was a time of trust in others.

News of wrongdoing in government or industry rarely became public knowledge, thereby creating a high level of trust that brought comfort and security. People believed that government and industry had their best interest at heart. Because the public was uninformed, gaining their trust was not hard.

Family units consisted of the mother, father, and children. Divorce was rare and carried a stigma. Many couples during this era who were not happy stayed together "for the sake of the children." Because of the low divorce rate, relationships were entered into with a high level of trust and security. The majority of young people believed that marriage was a lifetime commitment.

Graduates of the fifties knew a slow-paced, relatively secure childhood and teenage years. In the majority of households, the father was the breadwinner while mother was home raising the children. If a mother had to work outside the home, there was usually a family member available to be there when children returned from school; often a grandparent who lived with the family. Day care centers were scarce; children were cared for in a home setting. It was common for the extended family to live nearby, thus being an important part of a child's life, giving security and stability.

During the fifties decade, the suburbs represented the ideal place to live. Violent crime was infrequent in suburbs and towns outside of the inner cities. Murder, rape and kidnapping were rare, not a part of everyday news reports. Cars and homes were seldom locked. Children were not cautioned about talking to someone they didn't know; instead, it was considered courteous to greet passers-by when walking to school, waiting for public transportation or playing on front lawns. Parents were not fearful about letting children walk to activities or play in the park unattended. The suburbs were considered safe places to live and raise a family; there was no reason to have mistrust.

Radio, TV and movies were the basic forms of entertainment; more time was spent in personal interaction with neighbors and friends. Families played board games or cards, often inviting friends to join in. Friends and neighbors got together for coffee and dessert in the evening. Women enjoyed daily coffee with other mothers and their children. Summer evenings found people sitting on their front porches, exchanging greetings with neighbors passing by. A pleasant summer evening walk created interaction and connection with people.

It was also common to know the owners of businesses where people shopped—the bakery, butcher shop, drug store and hardware store, to name a few. Many of these stores were long-established family businesses; these merchants became good friends with their customers. There was conversation about family members, their health, their jobs, their activities. Because businesses were small, the customer had a feeling of personal connection with the store owners and employees; a feeling that someone cared about the products they sold or services they received. A more spontaneous, trusting feeling prevailed back then, reflected in people's warm emotional responsiveness as indicated by the writing slant.

Even in the cities, shopping experiences were more personal than today, as sales clerks were committed to making the customer feel valued. Anytime two clerks were engaged in conversation, they would immediately stop and offer assistance. Self-service did not exist yet, so when shopping, the customer had to work with a sales clerk, creating personal interaction. In the fifties, the customer was given special treatment; the motto of the business world was "The customer is always right."

Again, slant measurements of handwritings from the fifties show an emotionally outgoing inclination. This atmosphere of caring and connecting gave security, a belief that you could count on each other for support. The overall interaction of suburban, middle class society was to reach out to others.

The Sixties Decade

The sixties began as a continuation of the previous decade with some unrest brewing as public safety was being questioned with the publication of the book *Silent Spring* by Rachael Carson. When this book reached the stores in 1963, it sold in record numbers. Carson raised doubts and fears about the safety of the commonly used pesticides and herbicides. A review of this book brought to mind the slight scare that had occurred four years earlier. Just two weeks before Thanksgiving, 1959, Secretary of Health, Education and Welfare, Arthur Fleming, had warned the public against buying cranberries, a traditional dish for the popular holiday meal. A harmful pesticide had been found in a shipment of cranberries, so precautions were taken.

The public began to wonder how safe it was to be exposed to the chemical sprays used on crops and gardens. Was it true that our government and private industry would approve the use of chemicals that could possibly harm us? At first most Americans were reluctant to believe this unsettling information.

Another widely publicized book, *Fail-Safe*, written during this same period, was made into a chilling, thought provoking movie, of the same name, raising concerns over possible nuclear disaster. America had been engaged in a cold war with Russia since the late fifties, but the threat of a nuclear attack seemed distant until October, 1962, when we had the Cuban Missile Crisis. Some citizens began building bomb shelters in preparation for what many thought would be an inevitable nuclear war. Our country's sense of security was beginning to crack.

Back in the forties, secret atomic and nuclear testing began in remote desert locations. This now became a public safety concern as pockets of cancer started to appear in locations that would have been contaminated by wind currents carrying radioactive fallout from this testing. Media coverage presented information on these cancer outbreaks. The public was now becoming informed in a way that had never occurred before, weakening the trust that marked the fifties.

During the sixties the sensational murder of Kitty Genovese took place in a New York City apartment complex while people stood by and watched—but did nothing to help.

This raised questions as to why no one was willing to help her; were people too indifferent to care? As a society were we now making decisions to not get involved? This tragedy created enormous media coverage, which asked if citizens were losing concern for their fellow man, unwilling to act if someone's trouble didn't affect them personally. Across the nation, violent crime began making headlines more frequently than ever before. People feared crime would soon involve the quiet suburban lifestyle.

The Civil Rights Movement, begun in the late fifties, began turning violent. The assassination of the esteemed leader, Medgar Evers, in Mississippi shocked the nation. This horrible act was followed by more violence as the movement gained media coverage and public support. These years were a dark chapter in our nation's history. The Civil Rights Movement was long overdue; unfortunately the goals could not be accomplished peacefully. Young people would witness several years of violence and unrest before we would bring about needed changes.

November 22, 1963, added to the darkness the nation was experiencing. An assassin's bullets struck the enormously popular President John F. Kennedy as his motorcade drove through the streets of Dallas, Texas. Hours later, when learning the doctors were unable to save him, the nation was stunned.

The shock and insecurity increased five years later with the assassinations of two more prominent leaders. Civil Rights leader, Dr. Martin Luther King, Jr. was shot in Tennessee, and just two months later in California, Robert Kennedy, brother of the slain president was killed.

This senseless violence had a profound effect on the public. In 2004, Mark Kurlansky of the Denver Post called 1968 "The Year That Changed The World."

More insecurity came when corporations began the practice of transferring workers to various parts of the country as companies expanded operations. Transfers uprooted families as they were moved from one location to another. Children now had to adjust to a new environment, without the extended family nearby for support.

As the sixties drew to a close, public protests against America's involvement in the Vietnam War became a regular item on the evening news. Occasionally these protests resulted in violence or death. The country was now truly divided; young people were rebelling against government policies as well as many established rules of society.

The new style of media reporting, containing very graphic television coverage of the war, had to weigh heavily on young children; the security and idealism that prevailed in the previous decade was gone. Constant reporting of unrest, turmoil and discord ultimately breeds fears; fear affects the development of trust. We had become a very unsettled society. With the constant barrage of troubling news of riots, killings, and the war shown on TV, it wasn't surprising to see that handwriting slant was beginning to change.

The Seventies Decade

The beginning of this decade was marked by an effort to return to the "grass roots" stability the country once knew, a more settled time with hope that the turmoil of the sixties was over. By 1973, the Vietnam War had ended; troops were returning home to an environment that for many veterans was very hostile. Many people were angered with these veterans for their service in this controversial war; the disdainful treatment continued for several years. How different that was from the adulation and support the returning WWII veterans received. These new veterans sacrificed for their country and were treated with contempt; understandably they developed mistrust of their countrymen and the government.

Again the public trust was eroded when the Watergate crisis unfolded. Expanded media coverage provided in-depth coverage of facts that would not have been made public in years past. Detailed daily news reports continued for months until on August 6, 1974, President Richard Nixon resigned. Americans had always trusted their president; it was disturbing to learn that they had not been told the truth. This first presidential resignation in our history shattered what had been a high level of trust, a level of trust that has never been regained.

This decade saw an alarming increase in the divorce rate, rising **69%** since the mid-sixties. The social stigma of divorce had all but disappeared. Statistics showed that **40%** of children born in the seventies would spend some portion of their childhood in a one-parent home. The family unit as we once knew it had changed, contributing to feelings of insecurity and eroding trust.

The population became very mobile during this decade, as job transfers continued to increase. A job transfer often meant that a divorced parent was forced to move out of state, resulting in his/her being more absent in the child's life.

America's bicentennial observance, planned for July 4, 1976, carried with it the hope of regaining national pride and patriotism lost during the Vietnam War years. There was concern expressed that our society had lost the bonds, the cohesiveness that had once existed. Much hope was put on this celebration.

In an attempt to gain a more cohesive, bonded society, Sensitivity Training sessions were held. These sessions, conducted by professionals, took place in schools, churches, and work settings with the goal of promoting understanding and acceptance of our differences—just getting more "in touch" with each other.

The Halloween celebration of "trick or treating" was a long-standing tradition. It gave children a special time to dress up in costume, go out with friends, and collect candy. This fun-loving evening was forever changed when it was reported that some children had been given apples containing razor blades and candy laced with poison. The majority of these reports proved to be unfounded, but the fear that resulted changed the dynamics of this otherwise carefree tradition. "Trick or treating" would hereafter require supervision; parents became fearful about allowing their children to receive "treats" from anyone they did not know. Many hospitals offered free x-ray scanning of Halloween treats and parents were advised to carefully scrutinize all candy, making certain it had not been unwrapped or tampered with. These incidents sent messages of fear and mistrust to many children.

As the decade of the seventies drew to a close, President Jimmy Carter scheduled television time to broadcast his special message to the nation. In it, he voiced concern over what he termed "feelings of doubt" that now plagued the American people. He said that the assassination of President Kennedy, the Vietnam War, Watergate scandal, the energy crisis and the spiraling rise in the rate of inflation had left a mark on people, resulting in a disappearance of the unity and connection Americans once felt. He urged all Americans to work toward recapturing their old spirit of self-reliance, and to work together to rebuild the spirit of confidence and trust.

Graduates of this decade felt the societal influence that spanned the late fifties through the seventies. Change was occurring but not at the level that was to come.

The Eighties Decade

In spite of a growing affluence that allowed Americans to have more possessions than ever before, the general populace was restless, searching for fulfillment. Psychologists and psychiatrists alike reported seeing an increase in the number of patients treated for depression. They reported that many of their patients treated were troubled by an absence of a feeling of connection or closeness with others. A significant increase in the demand for personal counseling gave rise to the publication of numerous self-help books. A new format of television and radio programming known as the "talk show" quickly became a success. These programs gained instant popularity and were often called "a poor man's psychiatrist."

In 1982, the Tylenol capsule poisoning in Chicago served to heighten caution and mistrust. Tamper-proof containers soon appeared for food and medications sold to the public. These precautions serve as constant reminders that the trust we once felt when buying consumable goods can never be regained.

During the eighties, some couples chose to avoid the risk of a failed marriage by living together without the legalities of marriage. For many who chose to marry, signing a pre-nuptial agreement became a popular way to protect financial assets, reflecting caution that had crept into the culture, even with the most committed of relationships.

In the eighties, a new way of thinking had emerged, labeled the "ME first" philosophy. The message, geared toward young adults, was that one should make choices based on what the individual wanted, without considering how those choices would affect others. It was a self-centered way of thinking. Much concern was raised over this attitude—how would it influence efforts to return to a more connected, team approach, with people united and working together?

The cultural influence of this decade would impact those entering their teens—the future Generation X.

The Nineties Decade

The final decade of the twentieth century was an exciting one—a time to reflect on the amazing scientific and technological progress man had made in the previous fifty years. Communication was far superior and more sophisticated than ever, resulting in the times being labeled the Information Age.

But now that we can be in instant touch with people all over the world, do we feel a deeper, more personal connection with them? Much of our connection is now electronic rather than personal. A major airline once ran a TV commercial in which a company manager told his staff that too much of their business communications had become electronic, and that it was now time to make face-to-face contact with their customers again. With our quick access to enormous amounts of information, super-fast communication, and the demands of increasing business competition, workers were retrained to wear more hats, work harder and have less time to spend with others personally.

The majority of nineties graduates were impacted by these corporate business trends, involving practices that were largely nonexistent fifty years ago. Down-sizing, corporate mergers, outsourcing, buyouts, takeovers, and forced early retirement are commonplace now. Naturally they create insecurity and anxiety for employees. Uncertainty and instability in the job market, along with increased competition adds to the anxiety felt by many young adults as they seek employment. A more cautious attitude is reflected in handwriting with an increase of vertical and back slant.

By the end of the nineties, frequent media coverage of dishonesty, scandals and bribery had eroded public trust and the esteem that people in power once enjoyed. No wrongdoing escaped public scrutiny.

People wanted officials who sought the best interests of the nation, not their own self-serving agendas. Frequent reporting of corruption understandably resulted in the public becoming cynical: "You can't trust anyone anymore." This acute awareness caused people to lose trust in elected officials over this fifty year period. Perhaps the more informed we are, the more skeptical we become.

Logically the high divorce rate would affect the belief that marriage is the ultimate commitment to a relationship. During the nineties even more couples chose to live together, postponing marriage, even when children were born. Statistics show that graduates of the nineties have a fifty-fifty chance of experiencing divorce even though many of them had seen the pain of divorce among their parents.

Throughout this decade and the previous one, children had to be cautioned to be wary of people they didn't know. Today most children who sell items for fundraising come door to door with a parent or older sibling. In the fifties children felt secure enough to leave their homes and approach others without any need for protection.

In the nineties, when "drive-by" shootings became a threat to unsuspecting neighborhoods, this new random act of violence caused many to keep more to themselves. The Columbine High School tragedy shocked the nation in April 1999, leaving 12 dead and many wounded. Other school incidents followed as the century came to a close; school was no longer the safe place students once knew.

Many women tried to balance a career with being a wife and mother, while the majority of children were involved in extra activities. It was a rare event when the family spent evenings together. Television, video games and VCRs consumed more of a person's time than personal interaction with family and friends. Family dynamics were shifted from the traditional family dinner hour and evenings spent together to a more hectic, impersonal lifestyle, where family members were always on the go.

As the decade ended, crime increased. The dangers of carjacking, police imposters stopping cars with lone woman drivers, and identity theft schemes were prevalent. Anytime the public is made aware of increased criminal acts, the need to be on alert results in another level of trust being destroyed. Fear, mistrust, and uncertainty have reduced our willingness to get involved, to respond.

By the end of nineties, interactions had lost much of the trust, the personal connection that existed in the fifties. Efforts to recover this intangible quality have not succeeded. This more guarded attitude may seem natural to graduates of the eighties and nineties, this has been their reality, but those who graduated in the fifties, sixties, and seventies understand how different things are today.

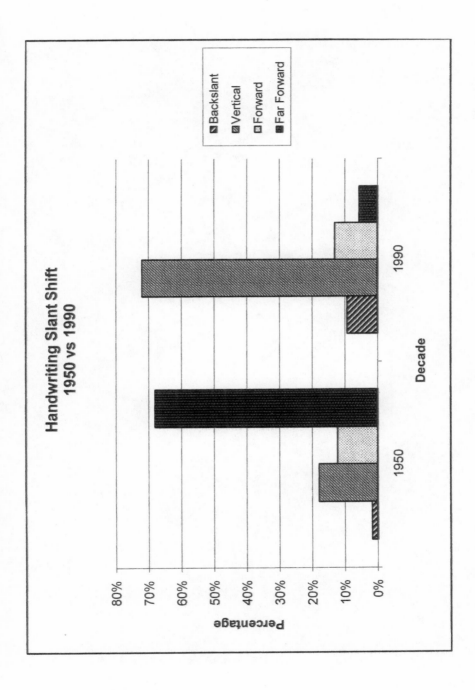

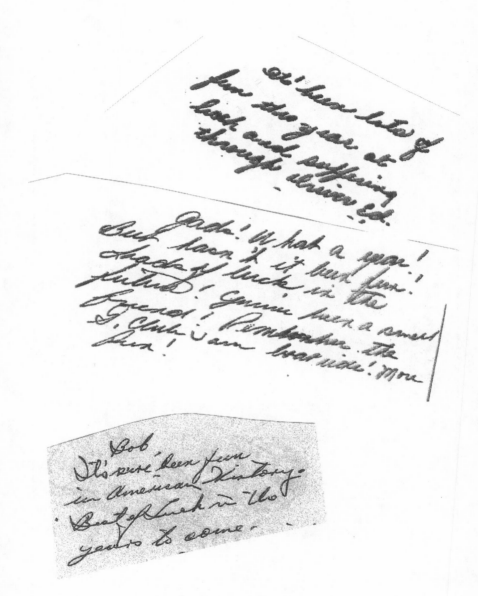

Fifties Yearbook

I'll never forget when you wrote "kick me" on my back. I'll never forgive you. Good luck in the future! We should hang out this summer! PARTY! I'm glad that mr. Martin is letting us graduate! Love always,,

newspaper has been great. We worked well together, and the paper was great. I'm so glad we worked well together. Your diligence and hunger to acheive will take you far in life. Have fun at BU and good luck with what you do in the future. Enjoy your time with Brett. He's a nice guy. God bless you;-

Nineties Yearbook

23

Chapter III

WHAT HANDWRITING SIZE REVEALS

To determine **size,** we must measure the height of the mundane area, which is the typical height of the small letters. Once the size of writing is established, it provides us with a baseline from which to measure other important traits.

It is in the mundane area where we see indications of the interaction traits such as communication, listening ability, mental processes, decision making, and attention to detail. The mundane area is considered an expression of self.

In this study I used three handwriting size categories:

SMALL SIZE

done

3/32nd of an inch in height or less

COPYBOOK SIZE

done

2/16th of an inch (the size students were taught)

LARGE SIZE

done

3/16th of an inch or larger

In scanning the many copies of yearbooks spread over my table, I quickly saw that the average size of student's handwriting had steadily increased over this 50-year span. How significant is writing size? What does it tell about the writer?

As I discuss the significance of handwriting size, the terms "small writers" or "large writers" will be used to reference the individual's size of writing, not physical stature!

The size of the handwriting tells us a person's habit in giving attention. Small writers focus more easily; large writers are easily distracted. Very small writers tend to focus intensely and can get lost in thought, unaware of what's going on around them. These writers prefer privacy and prefer not to be noticed by those around them. The smaller the writing, the more ability one has to concentrate on the task at hand amid distraction. These writers can be unaware of activity around them when working. Consider the case of two men who were talking to each other outdoors—neither of them was aware of other activity taking place in the field!

There is a natural tendency for small writers to be introverted and larger writers to be extroverted, although more personality traits have to be considered before we can evaluate that well. Small writers are more inner-directed, wanting to spend time with their thoughts, rather than having abundant social interaction. In a social gathering they are likely to look for familiar faces, and begin talking with those people. The large writer, provided he/she has reasonable social instincts, is more expansive and can mingle freely with people in a group, also having good awareness of people who are in the group some distance away. Large writers have a wide field of awareness of people and events going on around them.

Since larger writers are more easily distracted, it's natural for them, when in a group, to chat with one person briefly, and then another person they may see, and soon still another person who comes by. When you speak with smaller writers you feel you have their attention for some time; but in conversing with larger writers, you may see their eyes scanning the room frequently, taking in what's going on at some distance around them—noting who's arriving, who's leaving. Because of their scattered concentration, you may wonder if they have much interest in you!

Persons with very large writing enjoy being noticed. This desire to be noticed can be revealed in various ways, perhaps in the manner of dress, sometimes it is revealed in hairstyles or makeup. Life is their stage and personal attention is important for them.

Large writers want to be involved in larger projects; they dislike detail work. They like larger living and working spaces. Smaller writers should handle the detail work; very small writers can overdo attention to individual details and miss the big picture. They are content to have smaller homes and less expansive work spaces.

Let's take a look at how societal practices of the fifties could have affected handwriting size. At that time the writing taught in penmanship books was the copybook size, and yet, a smaller size writing was evident in **90%** of the yearbook samples I studied from that decade.

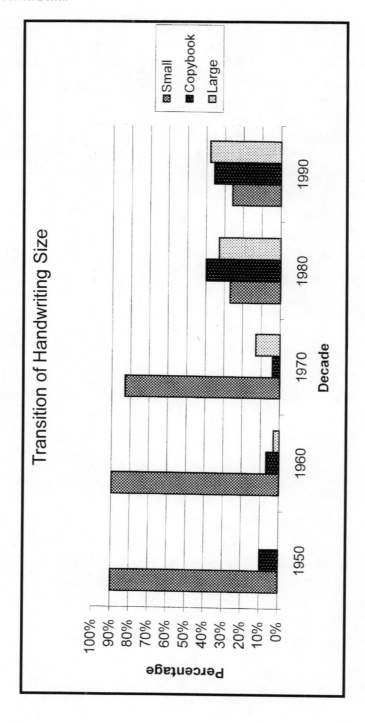

Not only did most of the fifties' samples fall into the small size category, but also the messages in yearbooks rarely took more than two to three inches of space. Larger messages were very infrequent, appearing to be limited to very close friends or that special someone. Was this a result of an existing belief that one should not take up too much space in a yearbook, but instead leave space for others to write in? This thought occurred when noting that most of the messages in yearbooks from the nineties contained messages using considerably more space on the page. Perhaps this noticeable difference reflected an entitlement attitude.

Graduates of the fifties were raised when cultural values dictated one should think of the best interest of others before acting. Children were expected to share classroom supplies and taught that you never took the last item, but instead offered it to another classmate. It was a time when children were criticized if they acted in a self-centered way. Feelings of entitlement and self-importance were not encouraged. The smaller size of their writing reflects this more reserved attitude.

Youth of the fifties were expected to perform tasks, concentrate on getting the job done without interruptions. Most students enjoyed any recognition they received and did not seek more; it was considered poor form if one tried to gain personal recognition. This probably resulted in most students preferring to take a backseat and blend in with other classmates. The small writer does not openly seek attention.

Educators tried to create an environment free of disruptions in the classroom with the belief that order, routine, and focus increased learning abilities. These children, who knew quiet study environments, showed stronger concentration in the teenage years; the percentage charts confirm this.

During this time, the absence of today's electronic technology kept daily distractions to a minimum. Movies were less intense, with a slower flow to the stories. TV programs were similar. Music, harmonious, relaxing melodies, was played at a lower volume. Even live presentations offered fewer distractions as stationary microphones limited the amount of stage area vocalists could use. The lifestyle tempo was slower, the absence of many environmental distractions resulted in most teens developing the habit of focusing well. None of the samples studied, from the fifties, contained writing which fell into the large size category.

As we approached the eighties, more advancement in technology became available to the consumer; video games entered the market. The popular Nintendo taught children to adjust to the game action amid the distractions created as the games progressed. These games required sharp reflexes and constant alertness, focusing required developing more awareness of the many distractions.

Contrast this with the slower, calmer, more methodical games of the past. Could these new, fast-action games have contributed to the development of a larger writing size, a size which increased during the eighties?

By the nineties, the business environment required people to deal with more interruptions; there was much more to handle than in the fifties. Let's look at a typical dental office as an example. In the fifties, the receptionist's job description was to answer the phone, file charts, schedule appointments, and handle billing procedures.

Moving ahead 50 years, the receptionist's job now required those same duties, but also entering data into a computer, preparing insurance claims for submission, submitting pre-authorization forms for recommended dental work, and handling insurance inquiries. Appointment scheduling became more complicated, as compliance with insurance guide lines was necessary. This increased work load created an atmosphere with significantly more interruptions. A small writer could find this difficult to handle, not liking to frequently break concentration on a task—and in fact concentration could shut out awareness of the new task that must be completed!

Today, continual interruptions are commonplace, requiring many workers to be adept at "multi-tasking," a term now on the list of qualifications employers are looking for. Did this ability develop as young people learned to adapt to the new and busier environment that technology was creating? Larger writing would reflect the ability to have a wider field of awareness—to become quickly aware of other tasks and interruptions demanding their attention for a while.

The workplace of today requires thinking bigger, thinking out of the box; such a different approach from generations ago. Pressures of competition have escalated; survival depends on being able to meet them. Large writers are good for getting the big picture, while it's good to have smaller writers on the same team, to handle the necessary details.

Large writers are "big picture" people; they don't care for tending to all the details which may be involved in a project. If they have to focus on details for long periods of time, their minds wander; they lose interest. They can switch focus easily and pay attention to something new for a time, but without good attention to details and good determination, they often fail to complete the original task.

The home environment, for those graduating in the fifties, included reading the newspaper, listening to the radio or viewing the limited programming on TV, reading a book, or perhaps playing cards or board games—definitely boring today!

Fast forward to the nineties; the home had TVs on, especially, with unlimited programming from 60 or more channels. Add in a VCR or DVD player, video games, the portable Game Boy, music from boom boxes, and the ringing of cell phones. Environmental noise has become a part of our everyday life, coming from external sources or a headset. As a society, we no longer seem comfortable with a quiet environment. We are living with continual intense visual and auditory stimuli, and young people today are used to it. Larger writing style shows ability to accommodate this modern lifestyle. It would seem to explain the **64%** decline in small writing size among graduates of the nineties.

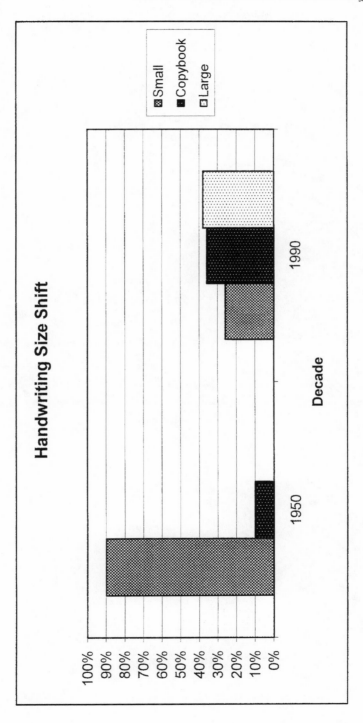

Its really been fun these past years. getting to know you better and all. I've really enjoyed every minute of it. Don't ever change, and be a good boy! ·

Well our last year is here. I have enjoyed knowing you. You have high character and a great personality. Best of everything you attempt, ·

Good luck to a swell guy, It's been fun in Jackson's room,

Fifties Yearbook

We have all been through so much together. I know that you and I have had our differences, but I will always love and respect you. You have so many talents and so much drive to accomplish things that I you can do whatever your heart desire. that with God's help we can all start to we always remember the wonderful times

NAKED, I WAS PRACTICALLY NAKED! I THINK THEY SHOULD JUST GIVE YOU A ROOM IN ELLIS HALL!

Nineties Yearbook

Chapter IV

DO WE HAVE A MUNDANE REALITY?

Writing samples were reviewed decade by decade. As I studied samples from the nineties a significant handwriting change was apparent—there was a decline in the probing of the **abstract** area of thinking. Thinking had gradually taken a more **mundane** (everyday concerns) approach. How is the level of abstract thinking shown in handwriting? Why do we care if abstract thinking has declined?

Handwriting is divided into three areas—**abstract, mundane,** and **material.** We will be concerned with the mundane and abstract areas only.

As explained earlier, the baseline represents the writer's here and now reality; each individual letter rests on a base line. As the pen forms a stroke leaving the base line, it may travel upward through the mundane (everyday concerns) area into the abstract (theoretical) area, or downward into the material (action) area.

The area immediately above the base line is known as the **mundane** area. This area represents the ideas governing our repetitive daily activities—the routines of daily living, including our communication habits. It also represents thinking in what we believe to be known, established areas of knowledge. Some letters, such as *a, e, m, n,* and *o,* lie entirely in this mundane area. Letters with upstrokes, or ascenders, such as *b, h, k,* and *l,* occupy space in both the mundane and abstract areas.

The area above the mundane area is the **abstract** area. This area is concerned with thinking and ideas involving principles, philosophies, spiritual beliefs, values, and theories. This is an area of thought where not everything is known; much is intangible.

The Written Script—Expression of Self

In learning to write, students were taught to form the upstrokes (often referred to as ascenders) to extend into this abstract area. The taller the ascenders, the higher the writer's mind tends to probe abstract thought and the future. The higher their reach, the farther from day-to-day reality the thinking goes. The tall, narrow upper loops seen in the writing of civil rights leader Dr. Martin Luther King, Jr., reflected his high values and idealistic thoughts. His writing exemplified long range planning, something lost today, especially for the majority of Gen X or Gen Y. Have we created this mundane reality for these generations, the future leaders of America?

On the other hand, when ascenders reach very little above the top of the mundane area, which is concerned with daily living and creature comforts, the writers operate by very pragmatic principles, caring mostly about what brings results right away in their mundane lives. Their abstract thinking reaches very little into the future; it gives limited thought as to what might be far-reaching consequences of their actions.

When young people are taught that they must live up to certain standards, a value system is formed that requires deeper thought about consequences before acting. This results in more use of abstract thinking. But if they are not taught these standards, then decisions tend to be based on what will bring immediate gratification, to bring more enjoyment to their daily lives. They base decisions on just a mundane reality.

To determine either abstract or mundane thinking patterns, the height of the mundane area letters must first be measured. Once their height is determined, the upper loops of the letters *b, h, l,* and *k* are measured against that mundane area height (the letters *d* and *t* are not included in these measurements). When these upper loops fall below a measurement of at least 2 times the mundane area height, it reveals thinking habits limited mainly to the mundane area, (a day-to-day philosophy). Letters which reach taller than that 2 times measurement show the writer probes the abstract area of thought, seeking knowledge, considering consequences before making decisions. The abstract area of thinking provides a vast frame of reference, more than when limited to the mundane.

ABSTRACT   **MUNDANE**

A review of past and present societal behavior and expectations will show how abstract thinking of Generations X & Y has been influenced. Percentages show an interesting shift since the fifties when societal pressures required most graduates to consider consequences before making choices and when the culture provided a stricter frame of reference.

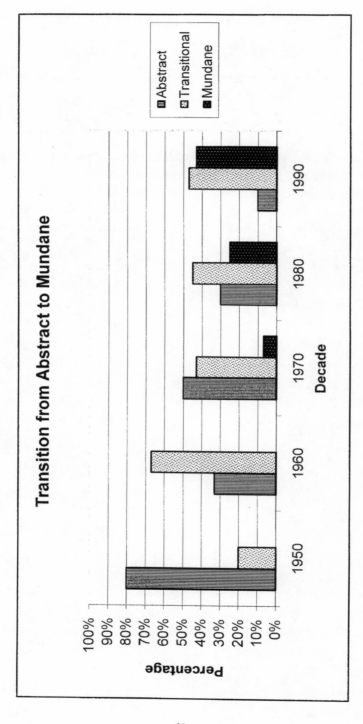

The Fifties Decade

In this decade, societal standards dictated guidelines for behavior, and were accepted by most without question or challenge. It was a time when great importance was placed on religion, morals, family values, and self-responsibility.

Prayer, silent or spoken, was usually observed as the school day began, as well as before sporting events, club meetings, and public ceremonies. History classes stressed the idea that our nation was founded by people with a deep faith in God; freedom to worship brought peoples of many faiths to America. Public acknowledgment of God was common; religion had an important place in society. Religion-based philosophy strongly influenced people, developing a pattern of abstract thinking.

The blessings of being an American were never taken for granted; they were continually stressed in the home, church, classroom, and the media. Our young, emerging leaders belonged to the "Greatest Generation," whose love of country was unchallengeable. This generation modeled a moral message to youth in their daily behavior.

Appreciation for the significance of our freedom, and acknowledging the many great sacrifices made to preserve this gift required deeper thinking. Emphasis was placed on the importance of American history, encouraging young people to ponder the philosophies, values, and dedication of our founding fathers. History classes stressed student pride and patriotism. Again, this required reaching into the abstract area of thought.

Abstract thinking begins in early childhood as the imagination is called in play to make pictures of what we hear and read. Graduates of the fifties spent much of their childhood in the thirties and forties, before television and video games were available. Children used their imaginations daily when listening to the radio, playing games, and reading books.

Before the age of visual image entertainment, games were created that made use of the imagination. Many childhood hours were spent just lying in the grass with friends, watching cloud formations taking various shapes that could be identified using imagination. Another favorite game was called Statues. A person was spun around, released, and would stop and hold a position until other players guessed what "statue" the person resembled. While these activities might be boring for children today, they served to develop thinking and imagination that reached higher into the area of abstract thinking.

The attitude toward spending money back then also stimulated the use of abstract, future-oriented thinking. High school students in the fifties were raised with a simple philosophy regarding expenditures—**do not make more purchases than the family budget allows.** Most households in suburban, middle-class America had to save for new purchases, a family vacation, or those unexpected expenses ("saving for a rainy day"). **The credit card was not widely used at that time.** Cash or check was the customary method of payment. The need to plan ahead prevented instant gratification, eliminating the more mundane approach.

These families held fast to the rule: If the income doesn't allow a purchase, you do without until you can afford to buy it. Sometimes expenditures became a family effort, with young people involved in the planning. Discussions were common as parents strove to teach their children financial responsibility. Since it was not possible to charge purchases, long-range planning was required to find extra money in the budget. Making a purchase required planning ahead, and therefore it was necessary to use abstract thinking.

Most adults chose to live within the budget and not borrow money from a bank, thus limiting purchasing options. Available was an interest-free payment plan, requiring the balance to be paid within a designated period, usually 90 days, or they could use a layaway plan. The layaway plan was popular with teens as they could make purchases after making a down payment, followed by a series of regular interest-free payments. However, the item remained at the store until fully paid for. Christmas Clubs were another resource, encouraging deposits into a savings plan during the year to build a reserve for Christmas spending, thus solving a financial squeeze that faced so many young people during the holiday season. All of these available options required future planning.

When students graduated high school and decided to become independent by moving out of the family home, they had already learned much about financial responsibility. Most parents of the fifties did not give their high school children money for purchases beyond the budgeted income. Children had to think past the moment, forgoing immediate gratification, to plan a strategy to get what they wanted further down the road. (It's interesting that a definition of maturity is the ability to put off immediate gratification for future gains.)

Personal responsibility was expected of students; good classroom behavior (graded as Citizenship) was as valued on the grading scale as academic grades. Disrespect of teachers, anyone in authority, brought punishment, a value taught and upheld by parents. When there are consequences for defiant behavior, people are more likely to think before acting. *This would require thinking beyond the mundane.*

Graduates of this decade were taught strict moral values at home; a rigid standard of conduct prevailed in society as a whole, developing abstract thinking. Parental influence on graduates during the fifties was extremely strong with little discord created from outside influences. Children and teens knew there were well-defined rules of behavior for all situations.

Entertainment media also influenced a significant part of a child's belief system by subtle messages conveyed. These high expectations of the fifties were upheld by Hollywood and reflected in the production of movies. Producers adhered to strict guidelines. No graphic sexual scenes were allowed, and no gratuitous violence or foul language appeared in the content of movies; a strong moral message was conveyed.

Hollywood celebrities were adored by their fans, a public who demanded they serve as role models; fans followed reports of entertainers' personal lives in popular movie magazines. When a big movie star stepped over the line, media coverage forced the star to take a back seat, avoiding publicity for a while. A much publicized scandal occurred in 1950 when a top star became romantically involved with her producer while making a film in Italy. When her resulting pregnancy was made public, she was banned from returning to the U.S. as a star. Criticism was so intense that Hollywood producers would not allow her to continue her career for years. Strict moral standards applied to all.

Television sitcoms, such as *I Love Lucy, Father Knows Best,* and *Ozzie and Harriet* carried a theme of morality and family unity dictated by these same strict guidelines. The scripts never contained even a slight suggestion that sex outside the bonds of marriage was acceptable.

Bedroom scenes routinely showed the couple wearing pajamas (often matching to stress the close bond of marriage), always sleeping in twin beds; sexual overtones were non-existent.

In the fifties it was socially taboo to engage in sex before marriage. What society considered "promiscuous behavior" was further discouraged due to a limited availability of birth control methods. Abortion was illegal. "Back alley" abortions were not a safe option; the risks were high. There were few choices for dealing with an unwanted pregnancy. The young couple could marry; however, the girl could not continue her high school education. When marriage was not an option, parents often sent the pregnant teen away for the duration of her pregnancy, putting the baby up for adoption before she returned home. It was considered unacceptable for an unmarried girl to raise a child. An out-of-wedlock pregnancy brought social disgrace to the entire family as well as to the young couple involved. Because of existing social stigmas, teenagers in the fifties had to give much thought to their actions; the consequences could be too great when acting on emotions. The strict moral code definitely affected thinking beyond the moment; writing samples from that decade show an **80%** well-developed abstract area.

The stricter the code of living, the more thought is given to one's actions. When a society expects conformity to certain standards, a deeper probing of the abstract area occurs as thinking patterns develop. A young person's values are formed based on accepted beliefs learned as a child that are modeled in the home and taught by the culture. When moral beliefs and values are part of one's philosophy, it requires one to probe the abstract area of thinking.

Historians refer to the fifties as a time of idealism and conformity. Both idealism and conformity are reflected in the taller, narrower upper loops of writing samples of this decade.

The Sixties Decade

The first half of the sixties was basically an extension of the fifties, with continued emphasis on religion, strong family values, and strict moral codes.

However, in the latter part of the sixties a change began, a growing number of college-age youth started questioning these values. As their voices gained strength, a revolution, dubbed the hippie movement, began bringing change to many established traditions. The voices of protesters demanded that long-accepted standards of conduct, morality, and dress be ignored. This movement gave rise to nonconformity. This was a period of social unrest with few constraints for those young people who chose to align themselves with these protests. The newly emerging social philosophy adopted the mantra "If it feels good, then it is right for you."

The existing moral standard that sex outside of marriage was taboo was soon to be shattered.

Women were encouraged to speak out and practice more sexual freedom. Helen Gurley Brown's book, *Sex and the Single Girl,* received notoriety when it challenged the concept of sexual abstinence for single women.

On college campuses, many professors encouraged rebellion against parental controls and society's strict standards. During this tumultuous time, long-standing rules and regulations were lifted in order to meet the demands of protesting student activists. Colleges and universities accepted this protest movement by making many policy changes, such as lifting curfews in the dorms, dispensing with quiet hours for study, permitting male/female socializing in dormitory rooms—generally abandoning traditional regulations. These massive policy changes had a profound effect on all students, marking the beginning of change for our culture. For many, parental guidance and moral values were now considered obsolete, not to be adhered to if one was to "discover self." Moral and religious influence on abstract thinking was diminished.

The importance of religion in our culture was also under attack. As a result of a lawsuit, prayer in public school had been declared unconstitutional by a Supreme Court decision. Bishop James Pike, a leader in the Anglican Church, publicly questioned the existence of God in his famous "God is dead" proclamation. Many college and university professors soon took up this cause as they openly declared agnostic and atheistic beliefs in the classroom.

This generation of college-age youth, known as the Baby Boomers, would become the parents of high school graduates in the late eighties and the nineties. Many high school graduates from the sixties were quick to join the protests in an effort to gain independence and experience personal freedom. The sixties have been named the "feel good" era, and these newly emerging philosophies would profoundly influence society in the years to come. Societal standards were soon to experience dramatic change!

The Seventies Decade

As the seventies began, most parents hoped for a return of more settled ways after the tumultuous sixties. They wanted a culture with more emphasis on family and a return to more traditional guidelines for society.

With a new, more permissive morality, the entertainment industry began producing movies containing explicit scenes of sex, graphic language, and violence; a definite departure from family entertainment themes of the fifties. Ratings were adopted by the film industry so the public would know the content of films. Parents now faced the problem of creating conflicts with their children if they restricted attendance at R-rated movies. For many, it was simply easier to relax parental standards and allow their children to see those movies containing questionable content. A majority of the parents, who eventually took the path of least resistance, reasoned that this was what society now accepted, so why have conflicts when it wasn't possible to control this. The messages movies sent played an important role in determining the values and morals that society was beginning to accept.

The birth control pill became available to underage girls without parental consent, allowing more sexually active teens. The Roe v. Wade decision of 1968, declared abortion to be legal, giving a new option for handling an unwanted pregnancy. The consequences of premarital sex had been lessened, the social stigma greatly reduced.

As a result of the student protests in the sixties, colleges and universities continued to relax rules governing students. Many campuses offered coed dorms with no regulations; conduct decisions were left up to the student. This freedom didn't give much pause for thought for many students, but it often made it unpleasant for students who still held to stricter values and principles. Young people were bombarded with messages encouraging experimentation with drugs and alcohol, now more abundant, easier to obtain. This appeal encouraged mundane choices with those seeking immediate gratification.

New, younger teachers began to come into the classroom, often expressing their moral views to the students. The power of their messages against the "old morality" carried tremendous weight in shaping the moral values of many students.

The Eighties Decade

As the eighties began, Ronald Reagan was sworn in as president. His overwhelming public appeal had been his conservative politics focused on the importance of regaining those values we appeared to be losing. A new block of voters, referred to as the Silent Majority, became a very vocal force influencing the election. They represented adults from all walks of life who were concerned with the more liberal direction our society had taken since the sixties.

In her effort to address an increasing drug/alcohol problem, the president's wife, Nancy Reagan, adopted a simple motto, "Just Say NO," in her campaign to raise awareness among the youth.

This decade began to place more emphasis on materialism, designer labels on clothing, ownership of products considered status symbols. The increased availability of credit cards made it possible to buy whatever a person wanted with little thought of overextending financially. Parents often incurred major debt in an effort to keep the image of being successful. Priorities, for many in the suburbs, seemed to be ownership of bigger houses and more expensive cars—mundane priorities.

At this time a new approach to parenting emerged—from the authoritarian mode to that of being a "friend" to their children. In past decades it had been stressed that children needed guidelines and discipline with love, not overindulgence, to feel secure. Now overindulgence and permissiveness defined the parenting style. Parents believed that to keep children happy, they shouldn't deny them anything they wanted.

Many parents no longer taught personal responsibility. Instead, they were quick to blame others for the actions of their child. Teachers were given less authority to handle problems in the classroom; parents pressured school administrations and teachers not to use discipline for behavioral problems. Students' rights soared while teachers' rights decreased. When children don't have to face consequences for their actions, they don't develop personal responsibility. Without personal responsibility, there is not much need to probe the abstract area for guidance. Personal responsibility is needed to foster maturity.

A most significant impact on attitude occurred during the eighties with the introduction of the *doctrine of moral relativism*. This ideology says we can't judge what is right or wrong using absolute principles— values or judgments should vary according to the situation and the culture. People decide what is "moral" for them. All beliefs, all lifestyles are to be accepted equally and should be tolerated. This doctrine gave rise to a new level of social tolerance and a decline in morality. Many colleges and universities quickly espoused this new ideology. Those supporting it argued that people should be free to choose their "values" and not be accountable to anyone else for their lifestyle choices. Moral relativism diminished God in society.

The Nineties Decade

The nineties saw more morality issues being challenged with acceptance of a more liberal attitude. By now, previous stigmas which labeled behavior as "good" or "bad" had vanished. Celebrities openly revealed their lifestyles—frequent divorces, extramarital affairs, living together and creating families without marriage. Gay and lesbian activists began testing the moral standards once they met with public acceptance. These cultural changes were slowly replacing traditional values. The "Silent Majority" of the eighties had lost its presence; those who questioned this new morality were labeled intolerant.

By the 90s, most movies contained graphic sexual scenes, violence and obscenity; the content of TV sitcoms frequently promoted a liberal agenda. In the early nineties, Vice President Dan Quayle became a brunt of derogatory jokes when he publicly questioned the message a popular sitcom sent to young girls. The show featured a financially secure, unmarried career woman who chose to have a baby, with no plans to marry. He stated that the show glorified unwed mothers and encouraged immoral behavior, a poor TV viewing choice for teenage girls. His stand resulted in constant public criticism and humiliation for him and his family. The lack of public support for his position gave another stamp of approval for acceptance of the new morality—mundane choices taking a new moral direction.

Public fascination with the private lives of sports figures and entertainment celebrities continued, as in decades past. Now, however, adverse publicity no longer threatened careers. Scandal seemed to whet the public appetite for more, and just enhanced the entertainers' box office appeal.

It was during the nineties that a significant change in parental role modeling took place. It became popular to depart from the traditional thought that single parents didn't live together, blending their families, until they were married. Instead, many moved in with their significant other or simply slept together each weekend without thought of the effect their behavior had on children living in the home. By acting on their own desires, did this behavior have an impact on developing thinking patterns as these children were forming a moral value system?

Does the church have as strong an influence on moral standards of society today as in the past? During the fifties, most clergy spoke out against societal practices that were considered Biblically immoral; a softer approach occurred during the nineties. Many Roman Catholics believe the disappearance of obligatory weekly confession lessened moral pressure on parishioners. Society's acceptance of a laxer moral code provides behavioral choices never condoned years ago, more choices based on a mundane, live-for-today philosophy. All of these new approaches served to affect the level of development of abstract thinking in youth of today; conforming did not require such a rigid conscience.

By the nineties, the focus to remove God from society became an agenda of some groups. This change began slowly creeping into society by prohibiting prayer at public events, removing Biblically based displays such as the Ten Commandments from judicial buildings in several states. The attempt to remove any religious significance from the traditional Christmas observance began with an outcry over Nativity scene displays on public property as well as banning singing traditional Christmas carols in school choral programs. These programs were now referred to as Holiday Programs, thus eliminating the phrase Christmas altogether lest there be any religious connotations. Religion has a profound effect on developing abstract thinking; when religion is diminished, development of abstract (principle-related) thinking decreases.

The reluctance to take responsibility for one's actions continued to escalate, having more societal impact than ever before. When someone was injured, it became popular to blame others (even when it was carelessness on the part of the injured person) and then initiate a lawsuit for large sums of money. By the nineties lawsuits escalated, suggesting a disregard for personal accountability among many. This "lawsuit happy" mentality discounted personal responsibility contributing to a rise in mundane thinking.

The affluent suburban lifestyles continued. Since the mid-eighties it had become common to give students cars for their sixteenth birthday; no responsibilities attached. Parents often picked up the expenses for insurance, gasoline, and car repairs. There was no need to develop long-range financial planning when one could enjoy these perks.

Handwriting samples of **43%** of graduates of this decade show a larger mundane area focus, with little probing of the abstract area, reflecting the attitude transformation Generations X & Y have undergone. The shift from strong abstract probing to heightened mundane thinking reflects a focus shift from pondering long term consequences to **living for the moment**, obtaining pleasure and comfort immediately. Does this shift in thinking (reasoning) have consequences for society?

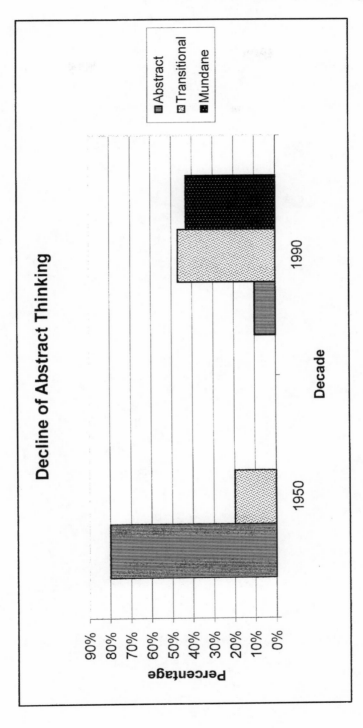

Bobbie,
I hope you
never will forget
all of the good times we
have had together as
Twirlers and as friends.

Good Luck
to a swell gal.
Hope we have as
much fun together
next year as we
did this one.
Love ya!
Barbara

Fifties Yearbook

So, have all your wild fantasies been fulfilled!? If not just call me up and we'll see what we can work out!! NOT Brian would kill! Anyway, summer is coming around the corner! What are your plans? Maybe I'll see your pretty face around! I'm going to come down for the last weekend in camp.

You are one of the nicest guys I know. You have so much going for you. I guess my best advice to you is live life to the fullest and always follow your ♡. I'm going to miss all your car advice, but if I do decide buy a new car—I'd look you up. Good luck to you and I hope you have a sucassyful future.

Nineties Yearbook

Chapter V

ARE YOU RAISING THE BAR?

When you take aim at something, the purpose is to hit the mark. Are you going to aim at something if you don't think you will succeed? Not usually. By using your thinking, you try to arrive at a decision on a goal. You review the facts and consider the situation, and then make a decision. Do you go for the goal or not?

Our thinking sets our goals in life. If the goal seems reasonable, we don't see obstacles and we have the abilities to achieve that goal, is there any reason we shouldn't give it a try? Sometimes we decide not to set goals we can achieve. Maybe we are overwhelmed with our present situation, underestimate our abilities, thinking we can't achieve that goal and so we don't attempt it, thereby avoiding failure.

So it is with the goals we set for ourselves; every day is filled with goal setting at some level. Our mental attitude is a big contributor to success. Having a positive attitude and believing we can do it is two-thirds of the battle. Even if we experience setbacks, strong confidence plus determination can get us there. But if we underestimate ourselves or are pessimistic, our failure rate will skyrocket. The ability to set goals and work toward them is necessary if we are to move forward in life.

Athletes competing in high jump determine how high the bar is set before competition; their success becomes a mental game before testing physical abilities. In the science of handwriting analysis, the placement of the *t*-bar on the *t*-stem tells the level of **goals** a writer sets. This is easy to spot when looking at a handwriting sample.

A person who sets high, ambitious goals places the bar high on the stem, and well above the tops of the small (mundane) letters. The lower the bar, the lower, easier, and more quickly achieved are the goals set. As in the case of the track competitor, achievement begins with an idea. Then action follows, as one seeks to realize that goal. Goal setting shows how much one feels secure in planning for the future.

When reviewing samples of the graduates of the nineties I was struck by a lack of high *t*-bars, a marked decline from samples of the fifties. What can account for this drastic shift over the past fifty years? Have we become so wrapped up in the day-to-day that we have developed our main focus on daily goals? Samples from the fifties showed that **80%** of graduates set practical to visionary goals, while only **7%** of nineties graduates did so. This would seem puzzling to note when we consider that the nineties graduates had many more opportunities to succeed than their predecessors. But then, why did so many writing samples indicate that they didn't want to think of reaching much higher than their comfort zone—the mundane area?

Let's look at the two categories of goal setting. They fall in to the range of high goals and low goals, each range containing two sub-headings based on the placement of the *t*-bar.

HIGH GOALS

VISIONARY   PRACTICAL

team   *team*

Visionary goal setting, indicated by the *t*-bar crossing at or near the top of the *t*-stem, shows that the writer is planning for a future time, goals are far-reaching. These distant or long term goals can be challenging.

Practical goal setting falls between visionary goals and the mundane area. The writer is willing to set goals that go beyond something that is finished today or tomorrow. The word "practical" means that the writer wants to feel sure they are attainable. As we noted earlier, goal setting of **80%** of the fifties graduates was in the high range.

LOW GOALS

LOW   MUNDANE

team   *team*

A *t*-bar which is just above the mundane area or even lower shows the mental habit of being concerned with just day-to-day goals; no real long range planning exists. A very low *t*-bar, set down inside the mundane area, denotes low goals, an indication of a lack of self-confidence. Failing to achieve will of course intensify this fear of aiming higher. Mundane and low goals represented the range of goal setting for **93%** of graduates of the nineties.

The setting of low goals can have many causes—complacency, boredom, lack of motivation, feeling overwhelmed. If one is content with the status quo, then there is no motivation to reach for more. Could it be that these students had not been challenged by those people who had influential roles in their lives? Cultural attitudes, changes in perspectives and the pulse of the country are other factors that undoubtedly influence one's outlook.

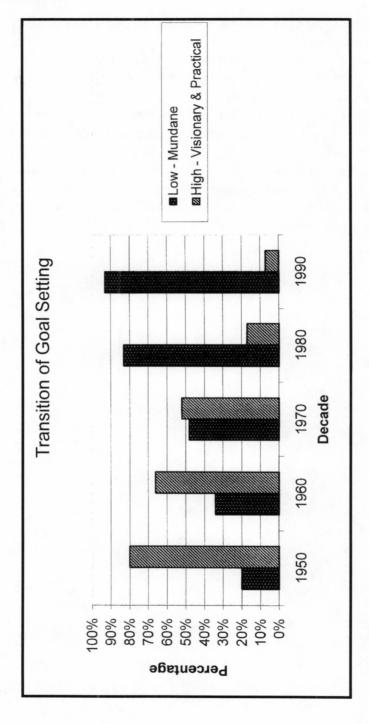

Noticeable declines in goal levels began to appear in samples from the seventies. It was during this period that the rise in suburban affluence began for many families, as credit cards became more readily attainable. Instant gratification became a way of life for children growing up with this new purchasing power eliminating the need to set goals and plan for purchases. For many Americans, the perception of long-range planning would change.

During the seventies, as consumerism increased, more products became available. Marketing campaigns were aimed at the most vulnerable consumers, the children. Successful marketing techniques gave children a vast range of products to look at, resulting in less satisfaction with what they already had. As they wanted more, parents bought more for them. Parents wanted to give their children a better life, keep them happy, and were able to buy more for them with their increased affluence. This was a time for many when materialism began to take over, often resulting in overindulged children. When children are overindulged by parents, it's not necessary for them to aim for goals they must work for—mom or dad will provide.

This new approach to parenting took hold and by the nineties, placating children with money and gifts was common practice. The majority of suburban families seemed even more affluent. Increased financial resources led to the desire to buy bigger houses and more expensive cars. The weekly allowance often became any amount young people asked for, perhaps $10 a day to spend on lunch or whatever they wanted; no work was expected in return.

The traditional concept of an allowance, earning money for chores completed, taught a work ethic. When allowance money was not enough, teens scurried to find jobs: newspaper routes, lawn mowing, babysitting, house-cleaning duties, as a means to acquire extra spending money for purchases not given them by parents. This made teens develop resourcefulness, and forced them to set higher goals—goals that would take a while to reach.

As suburban affluence increased in the nineties, one could see bikes, scooters, and many expensive toys left outside overnight on lawns or sidewalks, inviting possible damage or theft. In previous decades, out of necessity, children were taught to be more careful about their possessions. Because most families were not affluent, children learned that when toys were damaged or stolen, they weren't likely to be replaced. Learning to care for one's possessions teaches self-discipline and responsibility, necessary for setting substantial goals.

Childhood can never be happy at all times. As hard as it is for a parent to see children in physical or emotional pain, there will be times when children are upset by situations that are normal life experiences. How parents deal with these situations helps determine whether necessary coping skills that lead to self-confidence, necessary for high goal setting, are developed.

In an effort to make childhood a time free from worries, hurts, and disappointments, it became common for parents to deal with children's painful experiences by buying them gifts to avoid facing the upsetting situation. If children do not learn to deal with adversity, they do not mature enough to set goals for themselves. The teenage years are a time for maturing, in preparation for independence following graduation.

By overindulging children in our efforts to insure happiness, we hampered the graduate who someday had to learn how to set, plan for, and reach goals that took a while to achieve—goals that were independent of parental involvement. Many "empty nesters" saw their adult children return home to live because they couldn't live within their means and refused to change their lifestyle. This trend, called the "revolving door syndrome," surfaced in the nineties.

So far we've offered ideas correlating the decreased level of goal setting with cultural changes that took place during this fifty-year period. There are other factors that haven't been mentioned; namely, changes in the business world that could have contributed to this more mundane focus. It began near the end of the eighties when workforce competition took a new turn: job security was no longer what it once was.

As discussed in Chapter II, the uncertainty of the job market affected the level of trust seen in the writing; this uncertainty could also affect the level of goal setting. It's interesting to note that day-to-day goal setting, not long-term, is often predominant in the writing of top executives. Is this because competition is so intense, CEOs want to watch what the competition is doing right now, and be ready to react immediately with countermeasures?

The impact of the numerous societal changes could well have caused graduates of the nineties to feel more cautious and apprehensive about their futures. There is a lack of job security and more competition for jobs. Simply put, much more energy is required to meet daily demands of living today. Since energies must be more focused on day-to-day survival, there is less time and energy to make plans further down the road. Lower t-bars show energies directed toward the "here and now"—a day-to-day focus.

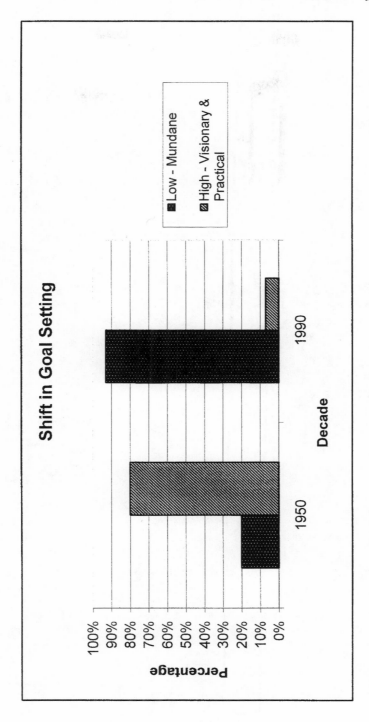

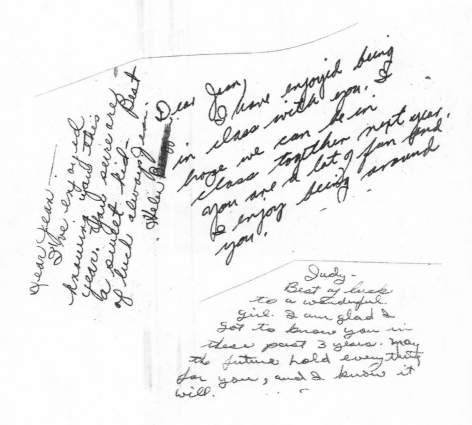

Fifties Yearbook

hance to get to know you
etter this year. I want to
ish you luck at DU - I know
ou will do well, but you have
promise me you won't get
ressed - PLEASE. You have so
uch potential and I know you
ll accomplish everything you want
do. You should call Lindsay and
we will try to do lunch (If you
en't working on any AP paper!!~

'Steve,
wadup dawg. I gotta admit,
I hated you at first.
It's a good thing (for your
sake) I got to know you.
Too bad your senior year of
football was the year before
we take state. Talk to

Nineties Yearbook

Chapter VI

PRIDE TAKETH A FALL

The trait of **pride** develops from a healthy desire for approval. It is natural for us to seek approval from important people in our lives; when our behavior gets positive feedback we feel good, and motivated to continue behavior that gains approval. In fact, we may put in extra effort, doing our best work in order to get it. Pride automatically regulates much of our behavior, preventing us from acting in ways that make us look bad in the eyes of others. Pride contributes to a feeling of self-worth. This desire for approval becomes more highly developed when society embraces high standards.

When children see pride taught and modeled to them, they are motivated to seek positive feedback for themselves and what they do. People with pride do not feel superior; they do not boast or brag. They just seek to do their best, holding high standards for their behavior and accomplishments; by meeting culturally accepted standards they feel self-respect. In Graphoanalysis, the trait of pride does not have the Biblical meaning of pride—excessive self-approval or vanity. Haughtiness is what is meant by "Pride goeth before a fall." Arrogance and haughtiness, not to be confused with the handwriting trait of pride, make people feel superior to others, perhaps even above the law, free to do what they wish.

If behavioral standards become open to individual interpretation, people are likely to not care so much to conform to them. For pride to remain as a character trait, conforming to high standards must be important to people. Loss of principles diminishes pride.

The trait of pride is found in the relative height of the stems of the letters *d & t.*

PRIDE

done

In the **d** we see pride concerning the writer's personal self and conduct.

Pride in the **d** is shown when the **d-stem** measures 2 to 2 ½ times the height of the circle portion of the letter.

team

In the **t** we see pride regarding the writer's accomplishment and performance.

The height of the **t-stem** will measure 2 to 2 ½ times the height of the mundane area letters, such as a, c, g, o, m, n.

Stems that are 3 times that height show *strong* pride, suggesting that the person has a special desire and need for approval.

Independent Thinking

When the height of these stems is shorter, a new trait is indicated, referred to as **independent thinking**. This differs from pride: the writer with this trait does not care about doing what is traditional if he/she sees another way of getting something done. *Independent thinkers set their own standards.* They are not necessarily rebels; they just reserve the right to do their own thinking. Others could say that they march to their own drummer. Many independent thinkers will act and present themselves in a dignified manner, just as people with pride will. They also enjoy getting approval; but when their way seems better, that's the way they will go.

If the traditional way works for the independent thinker, they'll follow it. But if a nontraditional way looks like it will give the desired results, they have no hesitation in choosing it—and they don't much care what others may think about it. In fact, you cannot get these people to change their mind on their independently conceived ideas unless they see reasons to do things differently. Only then will they change their thinking!

INDEPENDENT THINKING

done

As with the trait of pride, independent thinking in the **d** relates to one's personal self and ideas for daily living. The **d-stem** measures less than 2 times the height of the circle part of the letter.

team

Independent thinking regarding accomplishment and abstract ideas is shown by short **t-stems** measuring less than 2 times the mundane area height.

The shorter the **d** or **t-stem** is, the stronger the trait of independent thinking.

A combination of both traits was also seen in these handwriting samples. When a combination occurs, as it frequently does, pride serves both as a motivator and a restraint while the writer strives to measure up to high standards; independent thinking will lend originality, encouraging one to "think out of the box."

What role do events have in shaping our lives and influencing the development of these two traits? The following review of changing cultural standards over a fifty-year period will help us understand how societal influences contributed to the shift in the strength of these two character traits.

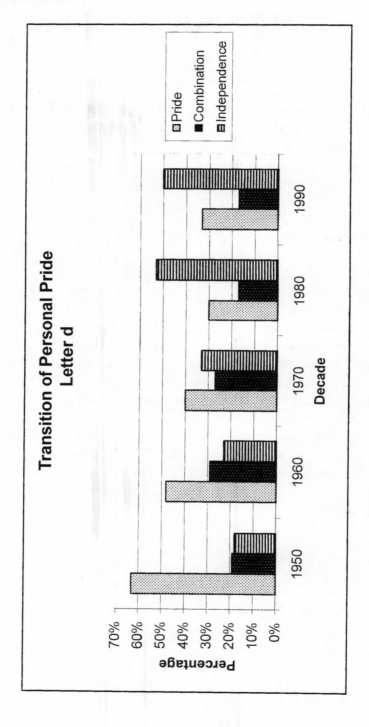

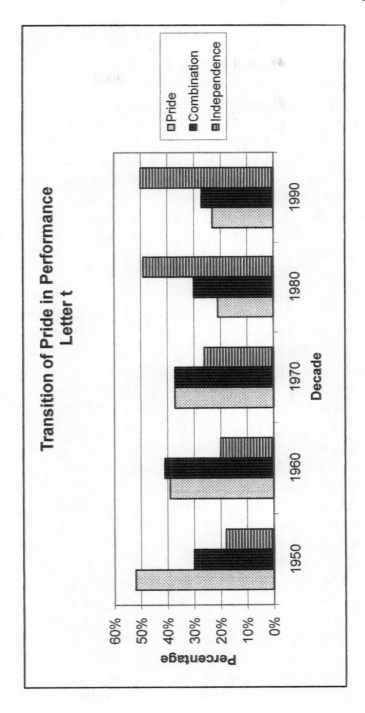

The Fifties Decade

When the fifties graduates were children during the time of WWII, they witnessed a nation fervently united in "the war effort." National pride and unity was shown along with daily awareness of the war on the home front. Citizens were called on to unite for "the good of the country" buying war bonds, collecting scrap metal and paper, while adjusting their lifestyle to wartime conditions. The war brought many shortages resulting in rationing of supplies; food, soap products, and gasoline. Despite the problems rationing caused for most citizens, they were not considered great sacrifices for patriotic Americans; sacrificing was considered a way for citizens to show their support for the men and women of our military. Working together for America fostered deeply felt pride. Demonstrations against our government's involvement in WWII would not have been tolerated.

After the war, America continued to feel and publicly display strong patriotism and pride. This continued throughout the fifties, when Americans were once again united—this time in the fight against Communism. Citizens believed that America was the greatest nation and all felt a duty to preserve this status. This was evident in everyday life. The Pledge of Allegiance was recited daily in every classroom, before sporting events and at the opening for school assemblies. Fifties graduates were raised in a society that modeled pride in our country, our government, our military, and our flag.

One of the highest honors for a young man, (women weren't yet admitted) was admission to West Point or Annapolis and beginning in 1954, the Air Force Academy. The standards of conduct for a cadet were extremely high; violations of these standards brought shame. Military academy cadets were highly respected and expected to serve as positive role models, showing integrity and honor. Scandals in these highly respected institutions seemed nonexistent; if they occurred, there was little or no media coverage, so the public was unaware.

In public, women were expected to wear a dress, high heels, hat and gloves, for men it was a dress shirt, tie, sport coat, and often a hat for social events. People dressed up for church, for travel by train or plane, even when going into the city to shop (shopping centers did not exist yet). One's appearance and attire was considered a representation of the individual, an expression of self-worth. The belief so often expressed was, "If you had pride, you took time to look nice."

In the fifties, guidelines for behavior were considered very important. Parenting style was authoritarian—children were expected to follow the rules without question. Children addressed adults using Mr., Mrs., or Miss, and were not allowed to interrupt conversation between adults. Good manners required proper etiquette; how to answer the telephone and take messages; proper letter writing techniques, even including how to address an envelope; how to respond to an invitation; how to greet people politely. When these guidelines were observed, a sense of personal pride was experienced.

Behavioral standards for teenage girls were strict and well-defined. Girls were taught that if they did not measure up, their inappropriate behavior would ruin their reputation, and hurt their chances of marrying a decent man (a husband who would respect and provide for them). This generation believed that women were dependent on men for their well-being, financially and emotionally. Conformity was needed for approval; pride in behavior was the result.

Society held high standards for everyone—young and old, businessmen, politicians, entertainers, sports figures; no one was exempt. Violating the standards could bring personal disgrace and shame which served as a control for behavior. One was constantly aware that he/she had to measure up. Pride was a strong motivator for graduates of the fifties.

Respect for others and their property was considered important; there was little vandalism. It was a disgraceful act to be seen leaving trash anywhere. True, take-out foods were not available but at that time people would have felt pressure to dispose of containers properly. Littering was not a problem; even the word "litter" was not part of daily speech then.

In the workplace, pride was a motivator to aspire to excel in performance. Employees felt that their workmanship and job performance was a reflection of their abilities. Likewise, in the manufacturing world, strong emphasis was placed on pride in the company's product. Corporations tried to manufacture the best product, so its identity would be synonymous with quality. The consumer demanded quality.

As a result, products manufactured in the fifties were built to last for many years; many even carried a "lifetime guarantee." Manufacturers coveted the Good Housekeeping Seal of Approval, a trademark begun in 1909 which became an endorsement of product quality, automatically increasing marketing success.

In the building industry, contractors and workmen took pride in what they built. Contractors held workers to high standards. Homes and buildings would last many years before requiring major repairs. Young persons entering the work force believed that doing their best work reflected pride, and with it came a measure of self-satisfaction. The fact that quality job performance would guarantee job security encouraged workers to go that extra mile.

Academic requirements were rigid, and these guidelines prepared students for high school graduation. During the fifties, America was a world leader in educational standards, and student achievement test scores were high. This legacy encouraged pride in performance.

The Sixties Decade

As the next decade progressed, the traditional standards and values, which instilled pride, began to come into question. Traditional family roles would change as a new feminist movement encouraged women to seek fulfillment in work outside the home; no longer was it considered a matter of pride or even commendable to be a "stay at home" mother. Now young women were being encouraged to step into new roles; independent thinking began to develop.

Feminism was one of the sixties' rebellions against societal standards. Others included rebellion against standards of conduct and dress; often the young people had sloppy dress and unkempt hair, making the older generation think they took no pride in their appearance.

As discussed in Chapter IV, colleges and universities were besieged with disruptive protests against long-standing rules and regulations. Pride was disappearing while independent thinking was emerging in those who chose to align with this rebellious philosophy.

Following the 1964 presidential election, the nation was divided over our involvement in the Vietnam War. Disrespect of the government grew with protests, even riots, with some daring to defile the flag. As a result of clashing philosophies, many patriotic veterans of WWII experienced alienation from their adult children. It was hard for older adults to witness these actions; it was conduct society would have never tolerated just ten years before, when national pride was very strong.

Unrest protesting the war continued to fester, and it erupted again in 1968 when the National Democrat Convention was held in Chicago. Politicians within the party were divided over the war and unable to reach any compromise. Soon rioting broke out, and the Chicago police had all they could handle. Did their behavior indicate a loss of pride, an absence of shame?

The decade of the sixties had a profound effect on the developing philosophies, morals and values of the Baby Boomer generation. Values formed during the sixties influenced parenting styles and belief systems that the Baby Boomers would pass on to their children, Generation X and Generation Y, who would graduate in the eighties and nineties.

By the end of the sixties, the trait of pride in graduates' handwriting was showing a **13%** decrease in both the *d* & *t* when compared with graduates of the fifties.

The Seventies Decade

This decade began with social turmoil carried over from the sixties, but it became more settled with the signing of the Paris Peace Accord in January, 1973, marking an end to the Vietnam War. However, pride in our country had not returned. War veterans coming home were often treated with contempt rather than being honored with homecoming parades and civic ceremonies. Pride in our country and our military was missing in a majority of our young adult population. Subtle protests, such as remaining seated during the playing of the national anthem, continued.

Prior to the seventies, most public schools had rules concerning dress. For instance, girls might not be allowed to wear slacks or shorts, boys would not be allowed shirts without collars or old blue jeans. Appearance had to be clean and neat; these guidelines were accepted by students and parents.

By the mid-seventies, changes in student attire became noticeable as more and more teens challenged these restrictions, wanting the right to self-expression. If school administrators refused to allow this freedom then some students, with parental support, went to court. This surge in independent thinking, going against long-held tradition, was upheld by court decisions which stated that students could not be required to follow certain dictates of dress. In the workplace, regulations limiting the length of hair for male employees were also declared an infringement of their rights.

The absence of dress codes seemed to permeate society; more casual attire was now accepted by the majority. No longer did people dress in their "Sunday best" to go to church; now a more casual look emerged. Many thought this represented a loss of self-pride and a lack of respect when worshiping God. The rebuttal for this was the argument, "it matters not what you wear; what matters most is you are there." Pride requires conformity to accepted precedent; independent thinking does not.

By the end of the seventies, handwriting samples showed that independent thinking, related to appearance/personal behavior, found in the letter *d*, had almost doubled among graduates.

Daytime vandalism began to increase in suburban communities. Police and citizens blamed high schools for adopting "open campus" policies. Open campus regulations allowed students to leave school grounds anytime during the day. Increased affluence provided many teens with cars they drove to school. Classroom attendance policies had relaxed, enabling many students to ditch class or drive through neighborhoods, perhaps doing some vandalism for kicks. It was also during this time that littering became a widespread problem. School grounds, hallways, public parks and streets were frequently littered. Did students no longer feel pride in their school and community?

As the seventies drew to a close, having pride in workmanship had decreased; frustrated consumers began to rebel against buying poorly made products. No manufacturing industry felt this drop in sales more than the auto makers in Michigan. As a result of poor quality control, many customers began to turn to foreign-made cars, looking for a better product. Had the general decline in pride affected workers and perhaps executives? No longer did the American automobile industry enjoy the respect it had known.

The Eighties Decade

At the beginning of the decade, President Ronald Reagan addressed the nation, stressing a need for all Americans to regain pride in our country, pride in our work ethic.

With the disappearance of dress codes from most public schools, teens enjoyed their new freedom. Boys chose a sloppier appearance, while girls dressed in a more sexually suggestive manner. The attire of many teens did not match what many adults thought was appropriate; their rebellious choice of dress reflected independent thinking as they discarded traditional values.

National test scores began to reveal what many educators had feared—America's student test scores were declining, falling behind many foreign countries. Public concerns about apparently lowered expectations for student performance, less accountability, and easier graduation requirements were ignored. This nationwide problem was addressed when Charlotte T. Iserbyt, former Senior Policy Advisor in the U.S. Department of Education, published *The Deliberate Dumbing Down of America*. Her reporting was an expose of what happened to cause the decline of what she claims was "the finest educational system in the world." Many educators fault the replacement of traditional (teaching the "basics") methods with the new liberal approach. If the quality of education has declined, are recent graduates in the field of education as prepared as those teachers who graduated prior to the lowering of standards? Have we lost the pride once felt by all as educational standards deteriorated?

As the eighties ended, society was beginning to experience many consequences from the acceptance of moral relativism. This belief would further reduce development of pride by removing any feelings of shame about one's behavior. Moral relativism, discussed in Chapter IV, downplayed moral principles and societal standards of conduct in favor of the "values" an individual chose. Since students were being encouraged to "march to their own drummer," independent thinking was a perfect fit for moral relativism; it eliminated social taboos. Pride was no longer influencing behavior.

In many manufacturing sectors an apparent lack of pride was now evident as small appliances of inferior quality began appearing. These products were not lasting longer than a few years; no more impressively long guarantees or warranties were being offered. It became cheaper to replace a product than to repair it; society developed a "disposable mentality." When the quality of a product no longer holds importance, an element of pride is bound to disappear in the workforce and the manufacturing process. What caused this decline? Quality was compromised further when manufacturing began the move to foreign countries.

The Nineties Decade

National patriotism and pride made a slight resurgence during the Gulf War but, as in past decades, it never matched the pride felt in the fifties. By the nineties, fewer people were observing Memorial Day by attending community observances or even flying the flag at home. Sadly, it was becoming just another holiday for picnics for many of Gen X and Y.

By the nineties, few public schools had any dress code. School administrators and board members continued to ignore parents, who requested guidelines, despite statistics showing that when dress codes were required students felt pride and scholastic performance improved. Testing revealed that students educated in our public schools showed poorly when comparing test scores with scores of students from other countries. The goals, set in the eighties by the Department of Education, had not been successfully met.

A lack of dress codes was never more apparent than now. Personal appearance was once considered to reflect one's character; a sloppy appearance in guys suggested a "lack of class"; suggestive dress in a girl made her "cheap and trashy." By now society seemed to accept any public attire; whether for church or picnics in the park it could all be the same. This relaxation of standards apparently created enough problems for the congregation of a large church in the West so that church leaders decided there was a need to have "suggested attire" for people who served as ushers, lay speakers or singers.

Just as standards for dress had deteriorated, so had an emphasis on manners and social graces. Manners regarding social invitations were no longer emphasized. For example, invitations to catered events, such as receptions, often went unanswered, requiring the host/hostess to follow up with calls in order to find out how many people were coming. Social etiquette, taught in years past, required responding to invitations out of consideration for those hosting the event. Pride once served as a motivator and people followed cultural guidelines of social graces; no one wanted to be thought inconsiderate.

A new form of music, "gangsta rap," gained popularity as teens embraced this new genre. Rap had lyrics expressing disrespect for women, profanity, violence, brutal forms of sex, and hatred for others. These recordings became instant hits and teens living in the suburbs were the largest consumers. How could pride be developed when their minds were filled with these lyrics?

Daily media reports contained sensationalism and scandals. A much-publicized sex scandal, involving coed cadets at the Air Force Academy, brought the following comments from a 1994 graduate regarding the traditional expectations for "high moral character" among cadets; "Administrators tried to address the character issue in 1992. Modern society and the historic culture of youth make promises to restore 'character' at the Academy a pipe dream." A personal friend, a former Academy staff member who had many years of personal contact with cadets, told me that when he retired in the mid-nineties, he no longer believed that an honorable work ethic was being shown by all cadets. He said he had noted a troubling attitude change among many cadets during the later years of his time there; he saw a slow eroding of values. Is it no longer realistic to expect today's cadets to act with the pride once required to live up to long-held traditions? To date, most cadets continue to display pride in their conduct; those who do not bring a black mark to this honorable institution.

Scandals; involving government, churches, sports, entertainment, and the financial world, became frequent news items. Regardless of negative press, many public figures continued in their roles never expressing remorse, apparently lacking any sense of shame nor caring about the influence their actions had on youth who viewed them as role models. This disregard was never more apparent than for the eight years, during the nineties, of President Clinton's term.

Parents who attempted to instill the traditional values in their children faced an uphill struggle in the absence of good role models.

The loss of pride in job performance became even more widespread, permeating all segments of the job market. From professional offices to construction sites, employers complained about job performance and attitude of employees, stating there was more interest in getting the paycheck rather than in the quality of one's work—doing the job well. The incentive to go that "extra mile" seemed to have disappeared.

Employees had their complaints as well, frequently saying that few employers were loyal to their workers anymore; they didn't seem as interested in quality work as in the bottom line, production and profits.

The homebuilding industry was an example; increased production at the expense of quality workmanship made it impossible for workers to take pride in their work when under constant pressure of time constraints and cost-cutting. Good workmanship was hard to find in houses constructed during the nineties which were not custom-built. A comparison of houses built in the fifties with those built in the nineties shows lower construction standards. Back in the fifties, quality materials were more available and workers exhibited a stronger work ethic. High standards of performance must exist for both employers and employees for there to be pride in workmanship and finished product.

Throughout the nineties littering was commonplace, seen in school buildings, on school grounds, in parks, along roadways, even in remote wilderness areas, evidence that many in our society had lost pride in their environment and respect for others' property.

During this fifty-year period, cultural acceptance of lowered standards has resulted in a decrease of pride as a character trait. Pride was a predominant trait in a society which demanded more from the individual. Pride had a positive influence on integrity; the weakening of pride was very evident as the twentieth century came to a close.

The rise in the independent thinking trait reflects how attitudes have changed. We became a society which embraced an "anything goes" outlook; individuals no longer felt pressured to conform to, or measure up to, standards. The acceptance of a "do it your way," and "I'll do it my way" philosophy allowed for personal choice free from pressure, free from concerns about "what will others think?"

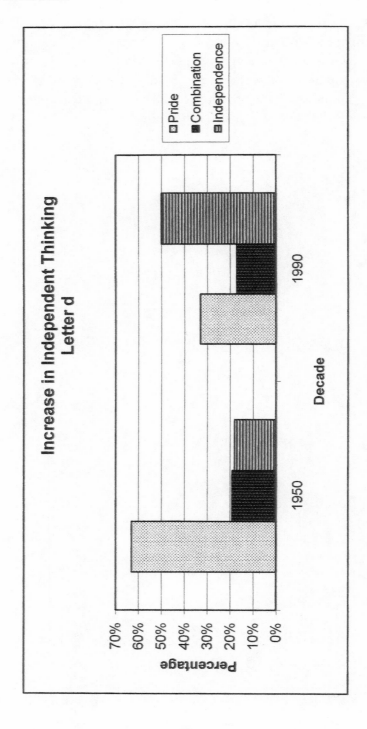

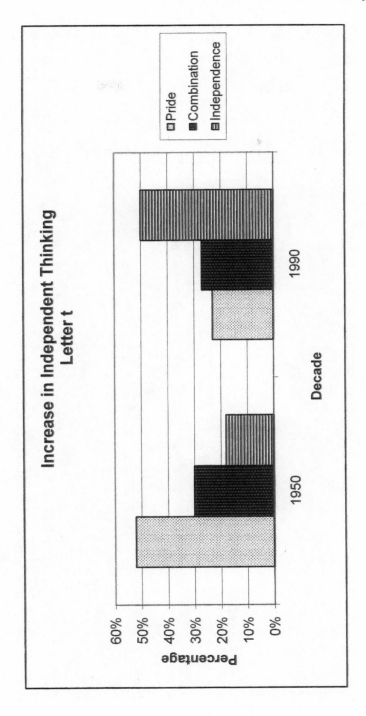

To one of the sweetest +
swellest gals I have known.
Remember all of the good times
we've had together. Best of luck

To a swell
Senior - we'll sure
miss you next
year - Good
Luck -

Sally -
It been a wonderful
year. been't it? It been
wonderful knowing you
this year too - You are a
very sweet gal - Luck always
to you -

Fifties Yearbook

82

Hey honey! Can you believe that this year is finally going to be over?! I'm glad that we've gotten to know each other better. You're the nicest guy in our school. You better call me all the time this summer!! I'm going to miss you when you leave for ~~Farm~~ (dress warm). you can just leave me all your summer clothes, OK?! Well, there's not much more to say other than I love ya and wish you all the luck in the world.

English has been fun but I'm glad it's all over! Your a really sweet girl. Good Luck next year. See ya later.

Nineties Yearbook

Chapter VII

SOCIETY'S MISSING LINKS

An easy to spot handwriting analysis trait is **generosity,** identified by the long, upcurving final strokes at the end of a word. The tendency to show these upcurving final strokes is a natural, due to the follow through motion, in penmanship but not in the printed form due to absence of connecting strokes; however, some printed letter forms can show generosity. For example, a printed letter *e* can show a forward extension as it finishes.

GENEROSITY

Came   came

Generosity represents one's desire to reach out to others to connect, a desire to share, to give without expecting to be compensated. It is the motivation to get involved, to offer help and act selflessly. If giving is intended for personal gain, it is not true generosity. As a trait, generosity is not commonly seen in handwriting, even though society recognizes that we should be helping others. It was once taught that "we are our brother's keeper"; unity was stressed when the emphasis was put on "being part of something greater than ourselves, acting for the greater good." These platitudes taught the value of working together, not just for personal gain. When a culture embraces a "ME first" attitude it does not experience that intangible sense of connection.

Handwriting is an "expressive gesture," an expression of the personality. Unless generosity is a character trait the writer possesses, it will not be present regardless of the writing style. When people have strong generosity showing in their writing it is reflected in their actions. We all know the person who offers help in times of adversity or just as a gesture of caring. This is not to be confused with the overwhelming response of citizens to a local crisis, natural disaster or a national emergency. These actions are wonderful responses that we as a nation have, but they are not proof of each individual having the trait or established *habit* of being generous.

As I studied samples from the nineties, it was evident that the trait of generosity was diminished; many samples from the nineties contained words whose final letters ended abruptly.

LIMITED GENEROSITY

came   came

Handwritings from yearbooks of the fifties recorded generosity in **67%** of samples, while yearbooks of the nineties had generosity in only **13%** of the samples. These shorter, often abruptly ending final strokes in the letter *e*, reflect the hesitancy to give more than one has to. This finding was not surprising, when considering the reduced responsiveness in the slant of today's writing, discussed in Chapter II. The more cautious attitude undoubtedly resulted from the decreased level of trust society has experienced, the increased focus on individualism, and the prevailing message to "look out for number one."

Much personal interaction has been lost in this electronic age once e-mails frequently replaced personal contact. Our over-structured, over-scheduled lifestyles have also resulted in a lack of time to interact with others. Increased workloads have been cited as making personal contact a low priority in spite of the various time-saving devices now available. Because free time is limited, everyone complains of feeling overwhelmed. Participation in civic and community organizations has seen a noticeable drop as people want more "down time," free from demands.

The handwriting from the nineties frequently had wider than normal spaces between words than it did back in the fifties. The meaning of wider spacing is that people want others to back away and give them some personal space.

This decline in social interaction continued to grow, while experts continued to offer solutions. One such plan was attempted in the late nineties when a newly planned community in Denver became one of many in the United States which were architecturally designed to bring people together. Homes were built around a network of walkways, encouraging people to abandon their cars and walk. These houses were built with front porches, with the hope that residents would spend more time outside interacting with neighbors, rather than secluded in their homes.

The entitlement attitude of putting oneself first has created problems for professions that work by appointment. Since the eighties, a reported increase in "no shows" or appointments broken with little advanced notice has created scheduling problems, while adding to operational costs. What happened to consideration and respect for other people's time?

This apparent lack of consideration for others is shown in the absence of responses to invitations discussed in Chapter VI. Once manners (society's rules of etiquette) were not emphasized as a behavioral guideline, personal interaction became more impersonal.

Doing business also became more impersonal once self-service became popular. Customers are on their own to find merchandise, then bring it to a clerk for purchase. It is not uncommon, when sales clerks are available, to find them engaged in conversation with a co-worker or talking on their cell phone, seeming to resent any intrusion should the customer request assistance.

A more impersonal approach has evolved with regard to hiring practices. Frequently, following an interview there is no further communication from the employer, implying that the individual has little importance. Today it is usually understood that if you don't hear from the employer, you didn't get the job. How impersonal compared to past years when one was always notified once the position had been filled.

Consideration, concern for others (placing value on them as you expect for yourself), must be felt if one is to show true, selfless generosity.

Scientifically, it has been proven that for emotional well-being, people need connection with others. Feelings of isolation can lead to depression, addiction, even suicide. Brain research has shown people are actually "hard-wired" to seek this connection.

By the end of the nineties, if someone was stopped on the side of the road, few drivers were comfortable stopping to offer help, or perhaps a ride into town. Due to the rise in crime, it is much more likely that people will restrain possible impulses to help, and drive on by. Feelings of compassion can now be salved with a cell phone call to bring help. Logic tells us that we are risking unknown dangers in stopping. Fifty years ago, when society was safer, people were comfortable with the idea of helping stranded motorists face to face.

Back in 1970, sociologist, Alvin Toffler, warned us that our culture was beginning to function on an impersonal level. In his book, *Future Shock,* Toffler made us aware of the traumatic affects of a transient society. He cited the emotional effects of continual change: "The greater the mobility of the individual, the greater the number of brief, face-to-face encounters, human contacts, each one a relationship of sorts, fragmentary and above all, compressed in time." Toffler stated that an individual experiences more people and change in a lifetime than ever before while maintaining our connection with each place for a shorter interval, resulting in more fragmentary human contacts with increased responses of withdrawal. We have been forced to make and break ties more rapidly. "We have all learned to invest with emotional content those relationships that appear to be 'permanent' or relatively long lasting while withholding emotion, as much as possible, from the 'short-term' relationships." Toffler refers to this as the "temporariness of the urbanization of society." Temporariness has an effect even when the individual does not move because friends, neighbors, and co-workers move, divorce occurs changing family dynamics, bonds are broken, never to be the same. Individuals have had to learn not to invest too much emotion in those possibly "short-term" relationships.

This impact, insecurity as the result of increased transition in our lives, is seen in the handwriting slant shift from a more intense level of emotional responsiveness to the more controlled vertical slant, discussed in Chapter II. The development of generosity is also adversely affected when emotional security is diminished.

What are we doing to repair this problem, knowing we are not feeling as closely connected with others as in the past? Pastor Rick Warren, addressed this growing concern in his book, *Better Together*, a sequel to his bestseller, *The Purpose Driven Life*. His message encouraged church members to reach out to each other, by offering help where needed. He stressed the need to become acquainted with people at work, with neighbors, and those at church, making connection with others, (generosity) a focus of their lives.

In an effort to promote more personal connections in society, Warren's book was widely adopted by churches as a guide for study groups. Throughout the country, churches with larger congregations formed Small Groups Ministry programs, with the intent of promoting more feelings of connection among members.

In previous chapters we reviewed each decade, exploring the potential impact that events and societal messages had on each generation. Trust and an inner sense of security must be felt before generosity develops. Personal experiences and societal influences are perceived as supportive or threatening, and will affect one's willingness to reach out.

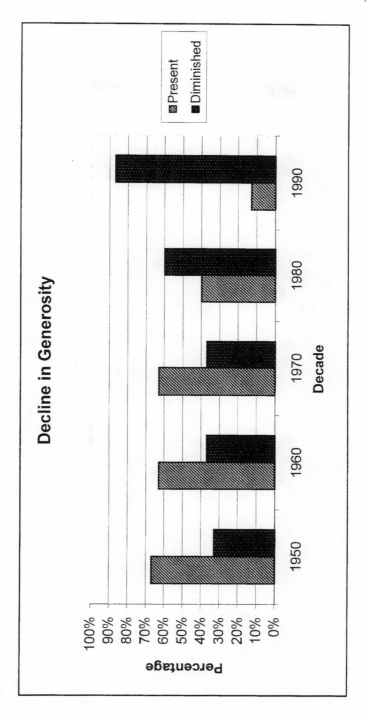

Hope you have all kinds of luck in your new type life and succeed in all you do. Be good.

Best of luck to a guy with a swell personality. Its been fun know you in 111. Don't ever change because your swell just the way you are.

Fifties Yearbook

Can you believe thats it's nearly over? 2 more days till high school's over forever. It's been a blast. Those Psychology skits were awesome. I hope you have a great summer

big guy. Even though we didn't get to find out who the best dunker is, we'll asume it was me! Good luck in ▬▬, I want to see you on the tube when I am sitting on my ass at CSU.

Nineties Yearbook

91

Chapter VIII

THE SELF-ESTEEM PUZZLE

How much value do we place on ourselves? We have heard the term **self-esteem** many times, but do we really have an understanding of what role it plays in our lives? How necessary is it for a person to have good self-esteem? Is this easy to acquire?

If you have good self-esteem you respect yourself. You believe that you are competent, have value as a person, are significant, and deserve consideration and respect from others. It is a feeling from within that does not depend on positive feedback from others. Good self-esteem produces confidence that one can somehow handle whatever obstacles come along.

It is natural to enjoy acknowledgement and praise, and to want acceptance. But with good self-esteem, the words of others aren't needed to maintain it. People with good self-esteem don't need expensive cars, designer clothes, a luxurious home, or other material possessions to establish their identity. They don't need to surpass others in order to feel superior. Healthy self-esteem is not to be confused with arrogance or egotism, an overly inflated sense of self.

Good self-esteem enables people to set boundaries for themselves. Teenagers whose self-esteem is solid are not likely to engage in self-destructive behaviors.

The teen years have always been difficult for people, a period when they crave acceptance from their friends. Today's culture entices youth with easy access to sex, illegal drugs, and alcohol, which can undermine and destroy their lives if they are not strong enough to avoid these risky choices. Yet they often fear rejection of their peers if they don't go along with them. Teens who have developed good self-esteem can find the strength to resist this peer pressure and make wiser choices.

The Graphoanalyst assesses **self-esteem** by noting the relative height of capital letters, especially the personal pronoun I, which I'll refer to as the PPI. The height of these capitals is measured against the typical height of the mundane area. Capitals ranging from about 2 ½ to 4 times mundane area height show good to strong self-esteem. Capital letters exaggerated in height (much taller than 4 times the mundane area height) suggest an inflated ego, one who views him/herself with a more superior sense of self (possibly from insecurity).

GOOD SELF-ESTEEM

When measurements barely reach two times that height, the writer experiences some self-doubt when comparing him/herself with others and could feel uncomfortable should the need to speak out in disagreement arise. The closer the capital letter height to the mundane area, the more fragile the self-esteem.

LOWER SELF-ESTEEM

In reviewing the samples, it was interesting to note that many writings from yearbooks of the nineties had a consistently shorter PPI measurement than did samples from the fifties. This data showed that a more secure belief in self existed among fifties graduates. This can seem puzzling when we consider that graduates of the fifties had not been exposed to school curricula promoting self-esteem; indeed there was little mention of self-esteem back then. In contrast, nineties graduates from early childhood were exposed to many positive messages, regarding self-image, from books, the media and school curricula. The new thinking was that continual praise would develop self-esteem, and educational curricula were redesigned to this end. But surprisingly, **30%** of nineties graduates showed lower self-esteem than did fifties graduates.

The most surprising statistic from the handwriting samples involved female graduates of the nineties. By a 2 to 1 ratio, girls registered lower self-esteem than their male classmates. Here was a generation of girls having new societal support, which told them that women could achieve whatever they wanted. These girls were part of the entitlement era—so why then did graduating teen girls of the fifties outdo them in self-esteem?

Back in the fifties, girls knew limited choices. Careers for women were discouraged. When a woman decided to work "outside the home," if she didn't have to, it was expected that she find a part-time job or one that was compatible with the role of wife and mother; a major career was unacceptable. And they were expected to give up their job after the birth of a child. During that decade society had well-defined roles—for men it was that of the "breadwinner," while "a woman's place was in the home." The employment sector favored men, making it hard to compete in a male-dominated environment. Women were given less pay for the same job.

The majority of high school seniors of any generation struggle with self-esteem issues. That is to be expected, since most of us mature well after graduation, spending years of adult life hopefully developing good self-esteem and the self-confidence which should follow.

If self-esteem is developed by positive messages of worth and encouragement, then what accounts for this discrepancy in the graduates of the fifties and nineties?

Do Struggles Hinder or Help?

Development of self-esteem is a complex process that begins in early childhood, involving factors that vary for everyone. The factors discussed here are but a few of the variables influencing this cardinal trait. We'll consider elements of today's culture that every graduate has been exposed to in some degree.

The belief that positive affirmations are important is correct, especially when combined with teaching a child self-sufficiency, resourcefulness, goal setting, and personal responsibility. Children must learn many of life's lessons before gaining confidence.

Confidence comes from success experiences. As children learn to cope with difficult situations, they gradually come to believe in their ability to handle them.

Graduates of the fifties had to learn to be more adaptable, more self-reliant, as parenting was less heavily involved, and not overly-protective as it became in later decades. Children back then found it necessary to resolve their own conflicts, and deal with their disappointments. Self-reliance is dependent on developing coping skills, positive ways to deal with stress, frustration and disappointments. It contributes to the development of self-esteem. Today's more affluent lifestyles mean parents can provide an easier childhood, so children may not be forced to develop resourcefulness and coping skills.

In the fifties, personal accountability was considered important; graduates knew their behavior would have consequences, with no adult ready to step in and rescue them or place the blame elsewhere. Parents, school personnel, and society were in agreement when establishing guidelines for behavior. Perhaps these boundaries gave a sense of security, because students were clear on what was expected of them—necessary for building self-esteem.

As the eighties began, public school educators began embracing progressive educational philosophies, which replaced the traditional methods of the fifties. The curriculum was redesigned to focus on developing the "whole" child, encouraging individuality, instead of simply presenting knowledge with a goal of intellectual excellence. The overwhelming majority of educators agreed that focus on self-esteem should be a primary goal, many new courses were developed with this objective in mind. Maintaining the belief that a failing grade could damage self-esteem, public schools soon changed their policies to reduce the chances of students failing. Did this lowering of academic standards affect the motivation to strive for excellence? Just as lowered classroom standards for school work hindered the development of pride, developing self-esteem appeared to be adversely affected as well. A positive self image is rooted in achievements, as students experience the pride of accomplishment.

Self-Esteem Cannot be Bought

Advertisements, commercials, and magazines portray good-looking, successful men and women, sending the message that they have self-assurance, but nothing could be further from the truth. Money, fame and looks do not insure healthy self-esteem. For years, media coverage has played up stereotypes for the ideal body, along with current fashions in hair and dress in every decade. Teenagers, especially girls, have always dwelled on their appearance, feeling that this was a key to their acceptance.

By the eighties, the self-esteem scores had dropped even lower. Many of these girls would fall prey to the new obsession with having a thin body as portrayed by the media. In an effort to feel accepted, they strived to conform to this popular image. In their search for self-esteem, many girls compromised their health in order to fit these unrealistic expectations. This obsession often developed into eating disorders, threatening health, sometimes resulting in death. Anorexia and bulimia became such a problem among teenage girls that in-resident treatment centers were frequently needed to help them recover, and gain a realistic perspective on their body image. Sadly, some could not be helped.

The nineties had ushered in a new value system, referred to as Madison Avenue values; they promoted the physical image and self-esteem connection more than ever. The obsession with physical beauty gave rise to surgical procedures intended to enhance physical appearance, appealing to women who were convinced that a more perfect physical appearance would assure their self-esteem. This cosmetic surgery is going strong today!

Can The Newer Approach Succeed?

Handwriting indicators throw into question whether the "ME first" philosophy and overly-protective parenting style has been successful. Statistical evidence from this study of handwriting changes give us reason to rethink some of the beliefs parents and educators have been subscribing to for the past several decades.

In the chapter on self-esteem in his book, *Why Kids of All ages Need to Hear NO and Ways Parents Can Say It,* Dr. David Walsh disputes many popular guidelines for parental interaction with children and teens. He suggests that *when children experience positive affirmations in combination with expectations of fairly high standards of performance and behavior,* they will be better equipped to deal with challenges, disappointments, and failures. And this will contribute importantly to the development of their self-esteem.

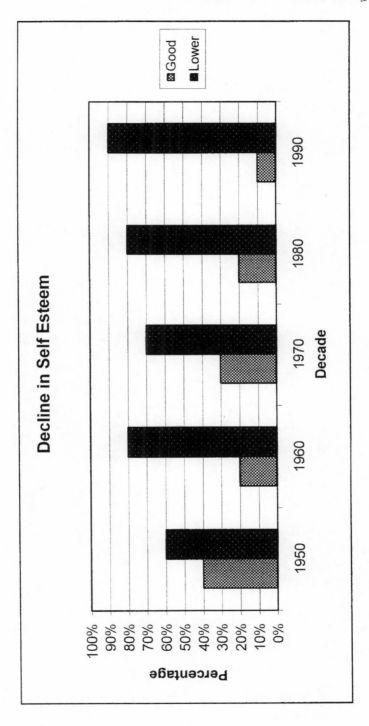

I wish the best
of everything in the future
It has been alot of fun
being in school with.
Good luck to you and
Chuck   Always

To one swell guy
I've had a lot of
fun going with
and being a friend
I wish you the best
of everything, now and
always.

To a really
swell senior. You
sure made a nice
football queen. I was
almost jealous that night
you know what I mean

Fifties Yearbook

100

It's been fun this year. Sorry for the harrassment this year, but I had to make marketing fun some now. Have fun next year at State & I wish you the best of luck.

I appreciate your friendship. I would Congraduations on all your accompli the best of luck in the future. Your w/ tons going for you. all of us hav Summer! Thanks for the great times will look forward to great times is

Nineties Yearbook

Chapter IX

STYLES HAVE CHANGED!

Handwriting, in its varying forms, whether cursive, print-script or printing, reveals the personality and character of the writer to those trained in the technique of handwriting analysis.

Elementary school children are first taught to print, and then to write and connect cursive letters forms. In the twentieth century, the widely taught forms of penmanship were the Palmer or Zaner-Bloser method. Each required concentration and much practice to master.

Students were taught to form each letter in a "copybook" style, following the models shown in their penmanship books. This writing was formed using conscious control. Once a child had mastered cursive and become more relaxed when forming letters, the penmanship began to depart from the pure copybook forms as the subconscious mind took over, expressing the individuality of the child.

ZANER-BLOSER WRITING STYLE

Penmanship Chart for the Classroom

Cursive was overwhelmingly the style of choice for **97%** of students in the fifties. Printed style was infrequent, sometimes requested for clarity, but otherwise seldom used. Engineers, architects, draftsmen, and chemists were required to master a special style of printing for their careers, however, at the end of the day when they wrote personal letters, most of them chose cursive.

The start of a trend, from cursive to printing, was evident by the end of the sixties. A small number of students printed their yearbook messages while another **10%** used an emerging writing style referred to as print-script. This writing is a combination of both cursive and printed forms, and eventually became favored by graduates almost as much as printing.

CURSIVE FORM

PRINT SCRIPT FORM

PRINTED FORM

The Decline of Penmanship

The typical explanation for the demise of cursive as a preferred writing style today is the reduction of classroom time devoted to teaching cursive, and the diminished emphasis on perfecting penmanship skills.

Graduates of the fifties and sixties can recall learning penmanship in elementary grades when hours were spent practicing tedious handwriting drills, good writing posture, and proper forearm movement and pen-grasping technique. Classroom time devoted to teaching penmanship today is a fraction of what it once was. Many nineties graduates have never learned how to hold the writing instrument correctly.

Adults over 40 can recall the elementary school experience of having to redo an assignment considered messy or illegible. This strictness disappeared in the eighties, as part of the new curriculum discouraging "red marks" on assignments, and the development of penmanship skills suffered because of the relaxed standards. Rather than requiring illegible work to be redone, using better penmanship, many teachers requested assignments be printed or typed.

By the nineties, many educators believed that future graduates would not need to master penmanship since cursive would become obsolete due to emerging computer usage and e-mail as a means of communicating. Penmanship would no longer be considered relevant in the 21st century.

Penmanship seems to be slowly becoming a lost art. Are there even many teachers today who have had adequate instruction for teaching it?

The Importance of Penmanship

In spite of the disregard for mastering this written form, there were some teachers who disagreed with the popular trend to overlook the importance of penmanship. They have not been willing to let this written form become a lost art; many have been dismayed by the lack of emphasis on penmanship skills. In the late nineties, Ed Boell, a third grade teacher in San Mateo, California, alarmed by the decline of penmanship, began encouraging students to use cursive for assignments, refusing to give extra credit for computer-generated work. In an effort to stress the importance of mastering penmanship and add a more personal touch, he suggested his students send handwritten notes to friends rather than use e-mail communication.

His efforts resulted in students writing faster, with greater legibility. This teacher demonstrated that developing penmanship skills takes time initially, but, when enough time is devoted to mastering this skill, writing cursive is easy because of its rhythmical flow. The teacher showed that cursive can be revived with a little extra effort in the classroom.

In the early nineties, Jeanette Farmer, a Certified Graphoanalyst in Denver, Colorado, learned of a study, completed in 1960 by Dr. Rudolf Pophal, a German neurologist and graphologist, which proved handwriting actually creates a physiological/psychological link in the brain.

Ms. Farmer always believed that practicing the old, traditional writing drills and techniques had a positive effect on the developing brain. These drills required much repetition and concentration, thus developing mental discipline. Her theory was that "push pulls" and "ovals", those drills so strictly administered long ago, aided development of neural pathways to the brain thought to improve impulse control, thus increasing the students' ability to concentrate.

She developed a program, *Train the Brain to Pay Attention the Write Way,* consisting of handwriting movement exercises, done to therapeutic music. This program is now used in selected schools in all fifty states as well as twenty foreign countries. Special education programs using this method report seeing significantly improved impulse control thus reducing classroom disruptions. Current research shows that handwriting movements shape and sculpt the brain as few things can. Her theory applies the same principles of repetitive movement used to reprogram pathways in the brain of stroke victims. Perhaps those daily exercises, stressed years ago, help explain why there were not as many disruptive students years ago as there are in today's classrooms.

Contrary to widespread belief, printing is slower than cursive, because it constantly has stops requiring pen lifts, thus reducing flow and speed. If properly taught, cursive is easier and faster to execute than printing, but by the end of the nineties, only **10%** of graduates were using the penmanship style.

What Does Printing Mean to the Handwriting Analyst?

Graphoanalysts and graphologists have numerous theories regarding the preference for the printed form, but to date no valid research has been conducted.

Handwriting analysts agree that the following statements are generalizations about the personality of the individual who prefers to print.

- Printing indicates a sense of self-protection when sharing feelings, and expressing emotions.
- Printers tend to have the same level of emotional responsiveness as the vertical writer.
- Printers stress importance on clarity in communication, they want to be heard.
- Printers strive to keep routine, it provides comfort and balance.
- Printers tend to be very involved in the present; they "live more in the moment."

The act of printing does give the writer a slight moment of pause before moving forward to the unknown future (and to people); it provides a subconscious control, deliberately slowing things down. The faster pace and lack of continuum in the society these nineties graduates faced possibly gives us further understanding of their preference for the printed and print-script forms.

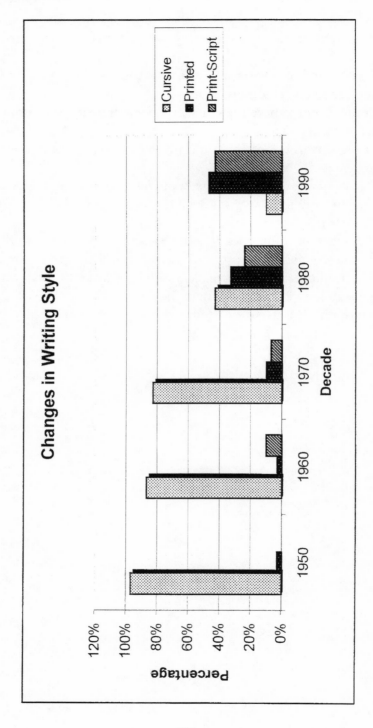

Chapter X

IS THE HANDWRITING ON THE WALL?

Where we've been influences where we are heading. A society relies on the past, for a frame of reference, to determine philosophies, expectations, and the culture of today. And these things determine its future direction.

As adults, we need to be mindful of how our choices will impact tomorrow—we create the legacy our children inherit. There has never been a period in history when a society was considered perfect, but as we decide to make significant changes we must look to the future with complete understanding of what the long-range impact of these changes will be.

The legacy we have created should give us cause for alarm, according to an article written by William J. Bennett, former Secretary of the Department of Education. In his article, "Does Honor Have a Future?" which appeared in the December 1998 issue of *Imprimis*, Bennett states, "Our culture celebrates self-gratification, the crossing of all moral boundaries, and now, even the breaking of all social taboos." Today, ten years after Bennett's article was published, we are aware of how these changes continue to affect attitudes, continuing the moral downslide Bennett addresses.

In the last half of the twentieth century, many changes influenced new generations. Today's attitudes will influence future generations. Handwriting analysis data has provided us with understanding as to how each generation was impacted during these decades. As the century ended, the most positive result of those fifty years was the emergence of a more tolerant society, giving equality to citizens once hampered by prejudices involving race or gender; those who aspired to achieve now had many opportunities. Those five decades also brought amazing advances in medical care and technology, and multiple new careers in the business world, offering endless opportunities resulting in vastly improved lifestyles. The American dream was available to all!

Considering these great strides, should there be any cause for concern? Apparently so.

In his book, *Death of Character*, Dr. James Hunter summarizes this period by stating: "The changes that have occurred are not just cultural. They have been accompanied by profound changes in the social environment in which children grow up. The increases in family instability, the absence of the father from children's lives, the number of hours children are left alone and unsupervised by adults, and the role of television and other electronic media of popular culture have all been well documented."

A Glimpse into the Future

As the twenty-first century began, the April 2000, headline of *F T Weekend* referred to the nineties decade as "The Age of Moral Confusion."

It has been nine years since that headline caught my eye, bringing awareness that those handwriting trait scores I had compiled held deeper meaning than simply a collection of interesting facts. This data served as validation that many societal changes had significantly affected the thinking of future generations, Gen X & Y. Those graduates of the nineties now comprise an adult segment of society ages 25 to 35, as they assume active community positions and become role models whose attitudes will influence youth.

The following article served as a reminder that attitudes resulting from the decline of higher standards (seen in the decline of abstract thinking and the loss of pride), are manifested in moral decline. In February 2001, scholar Charles Murray's article "Prole Models" appeared in the *Wall Street Journal,* addressing concerns about the coarsening of American life and culture. He said that Americans had good reason to worry about the unraveling of our society, with middle-class suburbanites accepting what was once considered low-class or trashy. In the past, self-pride would have prevented this because one feared disgrace or judgment from one's peers. He quoted Daniel Patrick Moynihan in saying that our culture was "defining deviancy down" by changing the meaning of "moral" to fit what we are doing anyway. (Loss of religious values plays a role here also).

Lessons of history remind us how moral decay can destroy a nation from within—it contributed to the downfall of the great Roman Empire.

The consequences of a slow deterioration of those principles once deemed important are evident if we only look around. What was once considered unacceptable behavior is now tolerated. Destroying a society from within can happen slowly, and like the proverbial frog in the kettle of water, society will feel comfortable until the water gets too hot, and then it is too late. Do we understand what has been happening and where we are heading?

Change Continues

A continued effort to remove religion from public life has contributed to an alarming number of young adults today who have never experienced a God-centered culture. If we are to return to the values once held important, we must restore religion as a foundation of our culture.

Lest we forget, America was founded upon principles of freedom to worship as people chose. Religion was a cornerstone of our government. John Adams, our second president and signer of the Declaration of Independence said, "The Constitution was written for a Godly nation; without God, there is no document or set of laws that can successfully govern people." William Penn, leader of the Quaker settlers, declared, "If we are not governed by God, then we will be governed by tyrants."

In addition to attempts to remove religious influence from society, it is believed there is yet another threat to our nation's religious foundation with the enforcement of "political correctness." This doctrine has become a concern to those who see it as a control over how we think, speak and act. An example of political correctness affecting public policy occurred in June 2008, when a school principal in Portland, Oregon, cancelled the Pledge of Allegiance from the year-end assembly because of its reference to God, a statement of faith that might offend any Muslims in attendance. Do decisions such as this deny our religious heritage and faith?

Without religious convictions and a disregard for higher values people become spiritually impoverished; America could become a secular society.

A New Outlook Sets Our Course

Are there indications the pendulum is beginning to swing back to more conservative values? Not according to the following news reports:

In March 2008, statistics from the Center For Disease Control in Atlanta, Georgia, showed that one out of every four girls between the ages of fourteen and nineteen has been infected with a sexually transmitted disease. Just a few days later, the topic of *Dr. Phil* was "Teen Sex," where it was reported that the United States has the highest teen pregnancy rate in the world.

In May 2008, a video titled, "Rape Dance", filmed to be viewed on an Internet site, was made in a suburban high school. As it was being filmed, showing students in simulated sex acts, faculty could be seen walking by, apparently ignoring what was going on. High school administrators and faculty were once expected to uphold behavioral standards, providing guidance. Do they no longer view this as inappropriate behavior or have they lost authority to act?

As the year ends, we learn that flirting has taken a new high-tech direction; many teens and young adults now use cell phones and the Internet to do this. A recent survey found that a third of young adults, ages 20 to 26, and 20% of teens interviewed have sent nude or semi-nude photos or videos of themselves to the opposite sex, "just to be fun and flirtatious."

Do any of these behaviors reflect on the lowered self-esteem of young women of Gen X & Y? Do these behaviors reflect the lowering of standards that have gradually redefined morality?

Loss of principles is apparent in much of society today. Change in attitudes can be seen in the greed and corruption that has brought disaster to our financial markets, large corporations and government. Because of the actions, of a few, and irresponsible financial policies, our country is experiencing a severe economic crisis.

Let's review just one aspect of this crisis that can be partly blamed on attitude changes discussed in this study—the sub-prime mortgage meltdown. Housing loans were made to anyone regardless of financial considerations. This practice began during the nineties and reached alarming proportions in September 2008. Numerous factors contributed to this disaster, but the main cause was unsound mortgage decisions, based on the desire for home ownership. Mundane thinking prevailed when home buyers and mortgage lenders focused on immediate goals instead of considering long-range planning. Sound financial guidelines were ignored when home loans resulted in buyers owing mortgage payments higher than their budgets allowed. Many of these buyers overextended their financial limits as they succumbed to decisions based upon instant gratification combined with mundane thinking.

The following statement, made by a young homeowner regarding the mortgage crisis, sums up the attitude of many today: "Someone needs to fix this financial crisis; I will lose my home if they don't— maybe Socialism is not that bad." Was it the government's fault that her mortgage was too high?

Out-of-control credit card debt continues to plague Gen X & Y. College students can't resist marketing appeals and keep their finances under control. Overspending is a major problem with college students; consumerism, not budgeting, has been their frame of reference. A bill before Congress would restrict credit card companies from marketing credit card offers to anyone under twenty-one. Most Americans, including college students, own an average of four credit cards. Credit card debt has risen drastically since 1990, nearing $1 trillion.

These financial problems reflect entitlement beliefs and the desire for instant gratification, attitudes that society has accepted for over two decades. Add in mundane thinking ("What do I want right now?") combined with loss of pride, which in the past fostered personal responsibility and it is evident that these attitudes create problems.

There is growing concern that liberal positions promoted by the majority of media sources and the growth of liberal philosophies in politics can take America in a new direction—possibly embracing Socialism. Gen X & Gen Y must begin to think about the future—try to use some abstract thinking—if they are to realize that people can't rely on the government to provide a comfortable lifestyle for everyone. At this time, due to the less demanding lifestyle they have known, it is difficult for them to understand how current attitudes will continue to take us further away from those values, work ethics, and standards that made America strong. Can we get things turned around?

Fortunately not all of Generation X & Generation Y have the attitudes discussed, but those who prefer to live by their own standards, content with their day-to-day reality, will continue to contribute to the direction society is taking.

Assessing Our Course

Gen X & Y represent a segment of the adult population whose votes shape our country's future. Are they taking this responsibility seriously? A November 2008, post-election survey revealed that a majority of these voters were completely uninformed about our system of government (many did not even know the number of senators from each state) and did not have any basic knowledge about the candidate they so ardently supported. All they knew were insignificant mundane facts, presented in negative press coverage, about the candidate they did not favor, such as, how much money had been spent on her wardrobe! For many of these young adults, their frame of reference lacks the solid foundation necessary to make prudent choices. This lack of discernment has been modeled by many parents and other segments of society.

Today, ten years after the Columbine High School tragedy, suburban statistics reveal that school violence, teen suicide, drug/alcohol abuse and teen sexual activity are even larger problems. Teens look to adults for leadership, for guidance. Have those persons in positions of influence provided the guidance needed for Gen X and Gen Y? What has America lost?

Our nation will always be dependent on the strength of its people for survival and stability; it is up to us to decide which direction we want to take.

This study reflects how each decade brought changes for our culture; changes that contributed to the attitudes of young people who experienced those decades. The change from the more conservative culture of the fifties to more liberal views today can be understood by retracing society's history. As a handwriting analyst, I understand how these trait changes affect personal philosophies and actions. Each one of us is the product of a myriad of experiences that shape our attitudes; handwriting analysis lets us see what has happened.

This handwriting study brought to mind the Biblical story found in Daniel 5:5, known to many as the story of the handwriting on the wall. Is handwriting once again giving us a warning? You be the judge.

BIBLIOGRAPHY

BOOKS

Brown, Helen Gurley. <u>Sex and The Single Girl</u>. New York: Random House, 1962.

Burdick, Eugene and Wheeler, Harvey. <u>Fail Safe</u>. New York: McGraw-Hill Book Company, Inc., 1962.

Daniel, Clifton, ED. <u>Chronicle of America</u>. Mount Kisco, N.Y.: Chronicle Publications.

Harms, Bill and Tilden, Janet. <u>The General Course in Graphoanalysis</u>. Chicago: Sheridan Press, 2001.

Lukik, Peg and Hoffecker, Pamela Hobbs. <u>Outcome Based Education</u>. Lafayette, LA: Huntington House Publishers, 1995.

Sowell, Thomas. <u>Inside American Education</u>. New York: The Free Press, 1993.

Toffler, Alvin. <u>Future Shock</u>. New York: Bantam Books, 1970.

Walsh, David. <u>Why Kids of All Ages Need to hear NO and Ways Parents Can Say It</u>. New York: The Free Press, 2007.

Warren, Rick. <u>Better Together: What On Earth Are We Here For</u>?. Lake Forest, CA: Purpose Driven, 2004.

NEWSPAPER and MAGAZINE ARTICLES

Bennett, William J. "Does Honor Have a Future?" <u>Imprimis</u>. Dec. 1998.

Geraci, Ron. "Get A Grip." The Readers Digest. Jan. 2008, pp. 107-111.

Goode, Erica. "Study: College Students Facing More Serious Emotional Issues." The Denver Post, 3 Feb. 2003.

Healy, Michelle. "Attachments Key To Improving Kids' Lives." USA Today, 9 Oct. 2003.

Jayson, Sharon. "Flirting Goes High-Tech, Low Taste." USA Today, 10 Dec. 2008.

Kourad, Rachel. "Cursive Being Deleted." The Denver Post, 9 June 2003.

Kurlansky, Mark. "The Year That Changed The World." The Denver Post, 25 Jan. 2004.

Murray, Charles. "Prole Models." The Wall Street Journal, 6 Feb. 2001.

Spencer, Jim. "Alum's Belief: AFA's Goal Unattainable." The Denver Post, 21 April 2003.

Weiss, Gary. "Don't Get Clobbered by Credit Cards!" Parade Magazine, 10 Aug. 2008.

Wilson, Craig. "Emily Post: How Rude Is This?" USA Today, 13 Oct., 2008.

RADIO and TELEVISION

Caplis, Dan and Silverman, Craig. Caplis and Silverman. KHOW radio, Denver. 20 March 2008.

Hannity, Sean and Colmes, Alan. Hannity and Colmes. Fox News Channel. Channel 42, Denver. 16 May 2008.

Ingraham, Laura. The Laura Ingraham Show. KNUS radio, Denver. 16 June 2008.

Kennedy, D. James. The Coral Ridge Hour. Channel 2, Denver. 14 July 2003.

McGraw, Phil. Dr. Phil, Channel 4, Denver. 3 March 2008.

O'Reilly, Bill. The O'Reilly Factor. Fox News Channel. Channel 42, Denver. 19 Nov. 2008.

WEBSITES

Farmer, Jeanette. "ADHD Ritalin and Kids." Retrain The Brain. http://www.retrainthebrain.com/penmanship.html (3 April 2008)

Iserbyt, Charlotte. "A Whistleblowers Account." The Deliberate Dumbing Down of America. http://www.deliberatedumbingdown.com/pages/book.htm
(1 March 2008)

Wikipedia, The Free Encyclopedia. "Generation X." http://en.wikipedia.org/wiki/generationX (4 Aug. 2008)

Wikipedia, The Free Encyclopedia. "Generation Y." http://en.wikipedia.org/wiki/generationY (4 Aug. 2008)

Wikipedia, The Free Encyclopedia. "April 20, 1999: The Massacre." http://en.wikipedia.org/wiki/Columbine_High_School_massacre (4 June 2008)

ABOUT THE AUTHOR

Sallie Ferrell Bolich is a graduate of Northwestern University. She received her certification as a Graphoanalyst in 1984 from the International Graphoanalysis Society. In 1999, she was awarded the society's highest honor, Graphoanalyst of the Year.

A portion of her handwriting analysis of serial killer Ted Bundy appears in the book *High Risk: Children Without A Conscience* by Ken Magid and Carol McKelvey. In addition to her speaking engagements and work with clients, Sallie enjoys a new endeavor, working with museums and genealogical research, using handwriting analysis to bring personalities of historical persons and ancestors to life.

Sallie makes her home in Broomfield, Colorado where she and husband, Don, raised their family.

Sallie can be contacted at: writeconsulting@gmail.com